Around The Horn

A Trader's Guide To Consistently Scoring In The Markets

Adrian F. Manz, MBA, Ph.D.

Stilwell & Company Publishing Group
Los Angeles, California

ISBN-10   0-9747653-0-9
ISBN-13   978-0-9747653-0-3

Printed in the United States of America

To my amazing wife Julie for being as beautiful inside as she is out. Your belief, strength and courage kept me going through the tough times. Your laughter, humor and spirit keep me going still.

To my mother Annamarie for a lifetime of support and inspiration. Without your unending love and kindness I could have never come so far.

And to my late father Friedrich for believing in me so strongly that I had no choice but to believe in myself. I know you would be happy.

Acknowledgments

Dave Mecklenburg for his persistence, belief, professionalism and friendship. Without his thoughtful editing this edition would not have been possible.

Peter Clinco because good advice and great friendship are hard to come by and you provide the best of both.

Gilbert Amster for his unconditional support and friendship.

Oren Raz who knows how to help a trader get his head in the game and keep it there.

Peter F. Drucker who taught me to open my eyes and see what is right in front of me.

Special thanks to Sean Katz of Scatter Design in Agoura Hills, California for creating a cover and layout that were exactly what I had in mind.

Contents

CHAPTER 1

Introduction

■■

When I sat down to write this book, I considered many methods of delivering the information that I wished to convey. My natural inclination was to write something technical with a heavy reliance on statistics and behavioral finance. The problem, as I see it, is that highly technical books often wind up displayed proudly on a shelf rather than being read to the point of being worn out. Since I would like the reader to profit from my methods, I chose to eliminate the technical jargon and instead teach trading using the metaphor of the great American sport of baseball to frame the discussion.

Trading and baseball share a similar history. They both started as relatively informal endeavors in New York and grew into massive institutions. Organized trading started under a tree along a wall that protected the city. The wall gave name to a street, and that street later became home to one of the most venerable institutions on earth. Organized baseball started in fields around the same city. Its popularity grew and it spread to fields around the country. As the crowds willing to pay a small entry fee to watch the game grew, so did the fields, until they became iconic institutions in their own right. Wall Street became symbolic of American capitalism. Baseball became the American pastime.

The parallels between the two endeavors run deeper than just their histories. Baseball requires that coaches and players use strategy in a game that, to the untrained viewer, seemingly does not require or lend itself to the use of any. The same can be said of trading. Baseball is as much about a player understanding himself as it is understanding the sport. Once again, this sounds a lot like trading. Professional ball players are known for their susceptibility to the influence of superstitions on their playing. If you don't see a parallel here, then you probably do not need to read any further. Finally, and perhaps most importantly, the greatest players in the game of baseball are remembered not for their records, but for their consistency. Ruth, DiMaggio, Gehrig, Aaron, and the list goes on and on. These players knew how to swing for the fences, but what really propelled them to the top of their profession was an ability to produce consistent results while avoiding mistakes. Find a trader with the same characteristics, and you have found a trader who is able to take profits from the markets day after day, year after year — bull or bear market, this person will survive them all and prosper.

My goal with this book is to teach the reader a consistent and conservative methodology for trading the financial markets. I have used the patterns presented for the past decade to generate consistent trading results. And I firmly believe that consistency is the key to survival in this game.

I know that no admonishment to the contrary will keep most readers from flipping first to the patterns, but I am going to give it a shot anyway. Becoming consistent is about more than just pattern recognition. A trader must understand his/her personal psychology, and develop a discipline that takes that psychology into account. Many books out there promise to teach you how to trade. I would say that this amounts to offering the impossible. Unless you happen to share the same life experience with the author, it is virtually impossible for a reader to glean enough knowledge to become profitable simply by reading a book. You need to teach yourself to trade. And part of the process of becoming successful is self-discovery. The sections of this book on Psychology and Discipline are there to help you evaluate yourself and to assist you in developing habits and behaviors that will allow you to profit from the methodology we employ in our own trading. I cannot overstate the importance of reading these core chapters in the process of applying the rest of the techniques in *Around the Horn*.

Around the Horn has taken on a life of its own since the first printing in 2003. Traders have embraced it and I am honored by the overwhelming response and continued support for the text. This edition has been updated with examples of the patterns at work through early 2007. The market is in better shape right now than it was at the time of the first printing, making the patterns even more consistent and exciting to trade.

That being said, the organization of the book is as follows:

CHAPTER 2

The Mental Game

....

…"I swing as hard as I can and I try to swing right through the ball. The harder you grip the bat, the more you can swing right through the ball and the farther the ball will go. I swing big, with everything I've got. I hit big or miss big. I like to live as big as I can."

— *Babe Ruth*

Most people flip right past any section on psychology in the trading books and periodicals they buy. Traders want information they can use immediately, and most importantly, make money with. We all look at the patterns first and hope that somewhere in the chapters that provide entry and exit techniques we will come across the ever elusive Holy Grail. Well, I am here to tell you that if it's the Holy Grail you're looking for, you have found it right here in chapter two. A trader's personal psychology, all the strengths and weaknesses he or she brings to work every morning, is the key with which the door to a consistently profitable career can be unlocked.

There is a simple fact with which every trader needs to come to grips; you will never master the markets until you master yourself. It will not matter how many books you buy, courses you take or personal coaches you hire. If you are not in touch with what makes you tick, the market will always be completely enigmatic to you. No amount of money, time or training will allow you to trade with anything other than the odds afforded to those who seek their thrills wagering on games of chance. The good news is that personal psychology is something people have been successfully coming to grips with and been able to master for ages. It is what makes any competitive, energetic and motivated person capable of fulfilling his or her dream.

A Ride Around The Horn

Great baseball players are masters of their sport in large part because they are self-aware. Of course they have athletic ability, but plenty of people who could not connect with the ball if their life depended on it have the same ability. The great players know their psychological boundaries and are masters of the balancing act that keeps skill and emotion working together instead of as opposing forces. They don't step up to the plate overconfident. They are not afraid to strike out. And they definitely don't keep a running total of successes and failures churning through their head. Instead, they strategize around their own psychology. That might mean trying to get many base hits and a high batting average, or swinging for the fences every time, knowing that this will result in a low average, but a potentially high number of home runs. Whatever the secret to their success, rest assured that it emanates from a confluence between the needs of the person inside and the actions of the person at the plate. The same awareness and psychological balance that make for a great ball player make for a great trader.

I think there are three general psychological road blocks common to struggling traders. They are overconfidence, a fear of losing and mental bean counting. We'll take a quick look at these. As you read the following sections, think about the impact each of these has had on your career in the markets. When you get to the point that each of these is held in check, you will find trading for a living to be a much more profitable and relaxed experience.

Can You Ever Be Too Confident?

If your mindset is one of overconfidence, then you will likely overtrade and decimate your return rate with high transaction costs. Research conducted at the University of California, Berkeley and the University of California, Davis found that overconfidence led to overtrading, with solid positions being closed in favor of less profitable ones. The study found that individuals who traded 45% more actively than their counterparts actually reduced returns by 2.5% per annum.

I believe that the solution to this problem is to trade according to a very clearly defined plan. By building discipline, traders can learn to avoid the pitfalls of constantly trying to fire off trades in an effort to beat the market. I can say from my own early experience in this business that shooting from the hip almost inevitably leads to shooting one's self in the foot.

I avoid overtrading by creating a detailed plan every night. This consists of one to six of what I consider to be the best trades for the next day in NYSE listed securities. When the market is trending, I don't see the excitement other traders do, but my returns are steady and my P&L heads in the right direction. When the market is tough, I still manage to keep a consistent rate of return. I am not in this business as a hobby. I am not in it for the excitement. I am here because I love trading and because my methodology allows me to make a living at it. I know traders who take upward of 200 trades per week and cannot even tell me what their rate of return is. They seem to enjoy the sport of it. I choose to run my business a different way. I know exactly what I will trade every day. I have a concise plan and a detailed log that I can review at a moment's notice. I know how my plan is performing and can easily ascertain why. I know the methodology works, and I can increase my dollar return at any time by increasing share size. This is truly the most beautiful thing about trading for a living. Once you have found what works for you, you can double your income simply by doubling share size. And you can do this over and over again. This is my comfort zone. I am inherently conservative, and this approach matches my psychology while providing me the opportunity to make a living doing what I love. Please be sure to review the actual example of a day of my trading plan and log in Chapter 15 after you have had a chance to become familiar with the patterns.

Do You Hate To Lose?

If your mindset is dominated by the fear of losing money, it is a virtual certainty that you will lose over and over again. Fear, like overconfidence, leads to cognitive errors which translate into trading mistakes. Fear of loss, not greed, is the reason traders stay with losing positions and dump winners. Although this seems counterintuitive, perhaps an example will convince you.

Say we have a trader whom we'll call Jim. Trader Jim takes both long and short trades and basically tries to follow a plan every trading day. Jim knows that trading is not an exact science, and that losses are part of the business. Nevertheless, like all of us, he would like to keep those losses as small as possible. Along comes a long trade in XYZ Corporation, which Jim takes according to his plan. The stock moves up, consolidates just short of the profit target briefly, and then moves sharply lower. Jim suspects that the trade is probably going to bounce. Since a bounce is not part of his plan, he exits the trade at the stop loss. He then cannot take his eyes off the screen. He watches in disgust as XYZ turns around right at the stop loss and begins to head higher. Jim is upset, but when XYZ trades through the entry price again, he takes the trade. This time, as before, the stock turns around and moves down to the stop loss. Jim once again exits only to watch XYZ reverse and move higher. Jim's strategy only calls for first and second entry, but the rest of his day is dominated by XYZ as he watches it trade higher and lower, with just about every exit looking better than his own.

So what has Jim learned from the experience? If he has balanced his psychological needs with the trading system he uses, then he is probably patting himself on the back for following the plan. If not, then what he has learned is that if he would have violated the plan he would have come out better for it.

This is the thinking that leads many traders down the road to disaster. They are afraid of losing. They fail to adequately address that fear in the construction of their trading strategy, and their entire career is dominated by it. If you find yourself letting losses run and cutting profits short, then you are probably allowing fear to control your trading. After all, profits feel good (rewarding) and losses feel bad (punishing). Thus, some will always take profits, however small, as soon as a position moves in their favor. I have seen traders take progressively smaller gains out of the market until a profitable trade barely covered commissions. The flip side is that losses are allowed to become larger, or even worse, are added to a portfolio of long-term holdings made up entirely of short-term losers. Why? Because not taking the loss means not losing. Thus the avoidance of the feared outcome becomes a self-fulfilling prophecy in which the ultimate result is the fear being realized in the form of emotional and financial failure.

Anyone Know The Score?

A great ball player never has a bad game — he just has games. Stepping up to the plate does not involve a mental recalculation of his batting average. It does not mean remembering the last time he faced this particular pitcher. And it certainly does not entail remembering how many times in the past he has struck out. The same is true of profitable traders.

To succeed in this game, you have to get to work every morning and be able to approach the markets tabula rasa. Fixating on previous losses will serve only to elevate the fear that prevents you from trading the plan. Focusing on a few days of big trades will bring out over confidence and over trading and turn a strong P&L into a fiasco.

I recommend not even counting your money. Obviously, we all need to draw our paychecks. And we need to remain aware of how our plans are playing out. But constantly counting the beans will not fill the jar any quicker. I look at my returns quarterly. Any shorter time frame, and I let performance start to worry me. And once we worry about performance, the game is essentially over.

SUMMARY

By any account, I have not covered the entire impact that personal psychological makeup has on decisions made in the markets. The three topics discussed here are simply those that I feel are common to almost all of us, and yet are almost never properly examined. We are all carrying baggage that fuels these and other problems in the field of trading. I strongly suggest that before reading any further, you stop to think about the roadblocks to success that you have erected, and the possible reasons and solutions for them.

CHAPTER 3

Ground Rules

....

*...The ability to win consistently without bending the rules of the game
is what separates the amateurs from the professionals.*

---- Anonymous

As far as I am concerned, the most important factor in becoming a successful trader is learning to stick to a plan. We have all heard the anecdote *"Plan the trade...trade the plan,"* but most of us find it nearly impossible to do so, even if we invested tremendous sweat equity in its construction. This chapter will lay the groundwork for developing plans based on the pattern entries detailed in later chapters.

Follow The Markets

It is entirely possible to trade every day without following market news at all. I don't know, however, that it is plausible to make a living that way. I know traders who will take a position in ABC, XYZ and everything in-between, yet are unable to tell me even the most basic facts about what makes the market tick. They have problems with their profit/loss consistency over time, and it tends to make them move constantly from one methodology to another.

In my opinion, a firm understanding of the broader markets is a precursor to success. As such, I follow a number of market statistics and plot them every day. These facts and figures tell me whether my trading plan is in sync with the market, or if I am relying on something out of the ordinary to move my positions in my favor. I construct my market barometer in both daily and weekly time frames. The format is simple and tracks everything that I feel is important to know. I use the spreadsheet in figure 3.1 as a means of consolidating the data.

Every trader should construct such a spreadsheet. Include the major market indices and a list of sectors that represent where the money tends to move. The sectors in my table are underliers of the majority of stocks that I trade. If my nightly scan begins generating frequent hits in sectors that I do not follow on this consolidated report, then I either add the sector or delete the stock from the list. My rule is that if I do not understand what the stock's sector is doing, I stay away from the trade no matter how good it looks. This ensures me increased odds of profitability over the long run.

As important as following the markets is, it is also critical to know what the indices are doing. By this, I mean that market internals must be examined to ascertain whether the markets are actually moving or if they are being moved by the great manipulators out there who profit by engineering runs on low volume. I follow basic internals such as advancers, decliners and volume (advancing and declining). I also follow the CBOE Volatility Index (VIX). This index provides a very good indication of whether the broader indices are going to sustain their current motion or reverse and head in the opposite direction.

	Mon	Tue	Wed	Thur	Fri
Indices					
Dow Industrials	12,423.49	12,416.60	12,442.16	12,514.98	12,556.08
NASDAQ 100	1,787.14	1,795.63	1,816.15	1,834.86	1,844.81
NASDAQ Composite	2,438.20	2,443.83	2,459.33	2,484.85	2,502.82
Russell 2000	776.99	778.33	778.87	788.45	794.26
S&P Futures	1,422.50	1,420.50	1,424.40	1,431.50	1,440.80
Sectors					
Airlines	60.48	60.97	62.61	64.57	65.27
Banking	403.60	403.02	402.42	402.93	403.36
Biotechnology	761.54	759.71	763.95	773.68	783.52
Broker Dealer	246.05	247.38	250.09	254.22	256.81
Chemicals	251.53	251.94	251.99	255.28	258.53
Computer Hardware	423.44	425.76	431.53	431.94	431.25
Computer Software	186.67	186.87	187.39	188.05	188.02
Computer Technology	814.50	819.08	824.11	830.79	835.92
Consumer	696.56	698.31	700.24	704.46	705.26
Gold & Silver	132.87	132.14	130.61	131.51	134.78
Healthcare	391.55	390.94	391.42	395.67	397.24
Healthcare Products	1,523.77	1,528.94	1,529.47	1,548.96	1,553.81
Insurance	391.51	390.04	390.96	392.75	392.92
Internet	200.05	200.17	201.20	201.68	200.21
Oil	623.04	613.01	602.94	598.79	616.63
Oil & Gas	1,134.39	1,116.22	1,097.28	1,092.86	1,126.96
Oil Service	186.46	185.12	182.66	180.30	185.41
Pharmaceuticals	347.59	347.53	347.43	350.37	352.70
Retail	496.95	501.04	504.32	511.93	513.84
Semiconductors	471.94	475.38	483.77	482.36	482.51
Technology	673.42	679.08	684.66	687.51	689.64
Telecommunications	929.79	914.78	917.89	925.92	927.56
Transports	4,624.18	4,632.66	4,641.47	4,693.04	4,760.27
Utility	483.67	484.20	485.46	484.68	480.70
NYSE Market Internals					
Advance	1,931.00	1,854.00	1,595.00	2,282.00	2,154.00
Decline	1,345.00	1,431.00	1,700.00	1,014.00	1,108.00
Advance/Decline	1.44	1.30	0.94	2.25	1.94
Volume	1,566,335	1,705,725	1,566,215	1,671,973	1,528,481
Volatility Index					
VIX	12.00	11.91	11.47	10.83	10.15
10 SMA	11.4	11.54	11.55	11.51	11.46

Figure 3.1 ~ Market Snapshot

Pick A Venue

I trade primarily New York Stock Exchange listed securities. While the patterns I rely on will work equally well in any market, I find the NYSE to be more predictable and easier to trade than the NASDAQ. This is not an absolute, and the choice should be made by each trader individually. Trade where you are comfortable. I know traders whose mantra is "if it moves I will trade it." If that works for you then more power to you. Just realize that the NYSE, even with the advent of the hybrid market, and the computerized markets are different animals, and each takes some getting used to. Each has benefits. Each certainly has drawbacks.

Using the NYSE OpenBook

If you plan to trade NYSE securities, then a good monthly data feed investment is the NYSE OpenBook which provides indication of the depth and liquidity of the market in any given stock. While not the same as NASDAQ Level II or TotalView, the OpenBook is less subject to gamesmanship, and provides a snapshot of what the market is about to do. There are some general concerns traders should remain aware of when using this tool.

First, the OpenBook provides only the data that represents the specialist on the NYSE. Thus, it can sometimes be out of sync with the Level II inside quote. This is particularly true in fast moving stocks with lots of ECN activity.

Second, the OpenBook represents only limit and marketable limit orders on the specialist's book. There is no indication of the number of market orders. Tape reading is still required if you are interested in knowing where market orders are located and where they are being filled.

Third, the OpenBook may be crossed or locked. If the high bid is above the inside ask, it will be placed at the top of the book in the order of greatest to lowest price. Offers that are placed below the market are put on the book in the same manner. Both types of orders stay on the montage until they are filled. This can be very helpful, since a large buy or sell order above or below the market will be reflected on the OpenBook, and not on the Level II screen, giving traders an indication of buying or selling pressure that is entering the market.

Fourth, short sales and stop-limits are reflected on the book when they are "elected" and are displayed at the price at which they are eligible for a fill.

Many NASDAQ traders find that they do not like the OpenBook because of the dissimilarities to Level II data. I would say just the opposite. I think that the absence of all the head fakes and market maker games makes the NYSE OpenBook more valuable than the its NASDAQ counterpart. I feel that, just like with any tool, you have to learn how to use it properly. Only then can decisions regarding its utility be made.

Figure 3.2 below shows the manner in which OpenBook data are displayed by the specialist. Note the presence of an offer of significant size priced below the inside bid. In the absence of a market order to buy 3,200 shares, this stock is about to move lower. I find that the OpenBook is generally pretty predictable in situations like this one. The bids at 56.48, 56.43 and 56.41 will be filled, some shares will fill as market orders between 56.40 and 56.48, and the balance of the order will move the inside quote lower to 56.35 x 56.40.

Bid	Size	Ask	Size
56.48	100	56.40	5800
56.43	1800	56.48	600
56.41	700	56.49	1600
56.35	200	56.51	300
56.34	100	56.56	200
56.32	300	56.60	500
56.30	200	56.64	200
56.28	100	56.66	1600
56.27	100	56.67	800

Figure 3.2 ~ NYSE OpenBook

Create A Scan List

In order to trade successfully, you must have a pool of stocks that will comprise a list of potential candidates. I create this pool every month and follow some very basic guidelines regarding price, liquidity and trend.

Price

I trade stocks that range between $30 and $120. This provides enough volatility to earn a living, and the requisite stability for my stops to be set within my personal comfort zone.

Liquidity

I construct my list of potential candidates to include stocks trading as few as 400,000 and as many as 4 million shares on average per day. I use a 30 day look back period to calculate average volume. I find that lower volume generally equates to better volatility and an easier market to predict. This is a personal preference, but you should definitely scrutinize this factor very carefully, as the personality of stocks trading less than 400,000 shares can be erratic, while those trading many millions of shares each day can be frustrating to deal with.

Trend

Almost every pattern I trade develops in the course of a trend. There are several ways to identify trending stocks, and I generally use the most simple of them. I look at the chart. If a line connecting the lows is moving from the southwest to the northeast corner, the stock is in an uptrend. If a line connecting the highs is moving from the northwest corner to the southeast, then the stock is in a down-trend. If the line moves horizontally from west to east, then the stock is not in a trend and should be avoided.

There are those who find this methodology too simple, or who prefer not to flip through a lot of charts every night. For those individuals there are several alternatives, the best of which is ADX, an indicator of trend strength, coupled with DI+ and DI-, which are indicators of directional bias.

ADX

Developed by Welles Wilder, and described in his 1978 book entitled *New Concepts in Technical Trading Systems* (ISBN 0894590278), the indicator measures the strength of an existing trend as well as whether movement exists in the market during one half of an ideal market cycle. I prefer a ten period ADX, while 14 is the number suggested by Wilder. A calculated ADX under 20 traditionally indicates a non-trending market. A move above 20 may signal the start of an up or down trend. When ADX begins to fall from a level over 40, it is traditionally interpreted to signal a potential flattening of the dominant trend. A very extended ADX can be used to indicate that the market is overbought or oversold, but I would advise against using the indicator for this purpose. Markets can maintain extreme readings for a long time, and a strong trend can continue moving indefinitely even if the ADX is well above 40.

DI+ and DI-

Given an ADX of 20 or greater, DI+ and DI- provide insight into which direction the market is moving. Generally speaking, if DI+ is greater than DI- and ADX is greater than 20 and rising, the trend is up. If DI- is greater than DI+ and ADX is greater than 20 and rising, the trend is down.

The derivations of the values are as follows:

High of the current bar = H
Low of the current bar = L
Close of the current bar = C
High of 1 bar ago = H1
Low of 1 bar ago = L1
Close of 1 bar ago = C1

Directional Movement (DM) must first be computed. To do this, we have to create a sort of tally for two teams. Label the first team's score DI+, and the second team's DI-. Now compare the current bar's high (H) and low (L) with those of the previous bar, (H1) and (L1) respectively. If $H - H1$ is greater than $L - L1$ then place the result of the calculation H - H1 in the DI+ column. If $L - L1$

is greater than H – H1 then place the result of the calculation L - L1 in the DI-column. Now total each column and divide by the number of cases to get the average.

Next, you must compute the true range (TR) for each of the bars. To calculate true range, take the greatest value of the following computations:

H – L
H – C1
L – C1

Using the same number of bars as you used for the directional movement calculations, (I use 10), sum the ATR values and compute the average.

Now, calculate DI+ and DI–

If DM was up, then $DI^+ = (^{+DM}/_{TR})$

If DM was down, then $DI^- = (^{-DM}/_{TR})$

$$ADX = \frac{(DI+)n - (DI-)n}{(DI+)n + (DI-)n} \times 100\% \quad n = \text{the number of bars in the look back period.}$$

Here, we divide the difference between all the DI numbers by the sum of all the DI numbers, and then multiply by 100 to change the value to a percentage.

As the ADX number becomes larger, the difference between DI+ and DI- will widen, and the trend on a chart will be in the direction of the larger of the two values.

While nearly every piece of trading software computes these values automatically, I suggest that you never apply an indicator to a chart unless you understand it well enough to explain to a friend how its values are calculated, and what the results tell you.

Scan For Pattern Entries

Once your scan list is created, you have the pool of candidates from which to draw daily pattern entries. Update the list as often as is practical, but no less than once per month. The patterns are detailed in the chapters that follow. What we need to establish here are the guidelines for determining entry points, initial profit targets and stop loss levels.

Entry points are at follow-through confirmation levels. I typically use .10 for stocks under $50 and .15 for those trading at prices above $50. Thus, for a long pattern entry in a $30 stock that requires a breakout above the previous session's high, the trigger price would be (H1 + .10). A short entry with the inverse requirement would trigger at (L1 - .10).

Entry is predicated on the fact that the pattern being considered seems to be likely to follow through to a profit target that is at least as great as the potential move to the stop loss. Determining this likelihood is where the art and science of trading collide, but the procedure I use can be roughly quantified as follows:

1. Examine the daily chart to see how much overhead resistance for longs, or support for shorts, will be encountered along the path you expect the stock to follow.

2. Examine the intraday 5 minute chart of the stock and determine if there has been significant support or resistance that might impede progress to the target.

3. Calculate the pivot, first and second support, and first and second resistance levels that will characterize trading on the following day (see next section).

4. Establish an initial profit target at or around anticipated overlapping support and resistance zones.

5. Determine a reasonable stop loss based on daily and intraday support and resistance confluence areas

6. Compare the prices in steps 1 - 3. If there is significant overlap of values in

the path to your profit target, discard the pattern for the following trading day. It is far better to just let a setup go than to try and reason your way through significant price inflection points.

7.   If there does not seem to be a significant obstacle en route to the target, journalize the potential trade and define the parameters on paper for the next trading day.

Calculating Pivot Lines

Each night, we identify market inflection levels known as pivot points. These represent the equilibrium areas around which most of the day's trading activity can be expected to occur. Statistically, a trader has a significantly higher probability of achieving profits when taking the pivot levels into account in assessing technical setups. Let's examine the calculations and what each point means.

The Pivot Point (P) is the non-weighted average of yesterday's price action. I refer to P as being non-weighted because the calculation is simply (High+Low+Close)/3. By contrast, the Volume Weighted Average Price (VWAP) is a calculation that is weighted to reflect all of the day's market action at every conceivable price level. Nevertheless, P is very important for a number of reasons. First, floor traders and market makers use P as a sort of axis around which to base fair price. Second if the market begins to defy this level as equilibrium price, its value is critical in developing the support and resistance calculations that floor traders will use to make their markets.

The first level of resistance (R1) is calculated as [(2 x P)-L], while the first support (S1) is [(2 x P)-H]. The results of these calculations provide a set of bands within which floor traders will anticipate containment of price. Price action in the absence of significant news events, within these bands represents the "value" range. Any move that penetrates one of these is what we commonly refer to as a breakout. When this range expansion occurs, off-floor intraday traders become interested and are pulled into the market. The level of activity here determines whether the move will continue to expand, or fizzle.

The second Level of Resistance (R2) is calculated as $[P + (R1 - S1)]$, while the second support (S2) is $[P - (R1-S1)]$. These parameters serve to generate a second set of bands, which will, theoretically, contain the newly expanded price action. If a move through these levels is achieved, swing and longer-term traders will be drawn into the market. The level of participation here can result in very significant breakouts, or once again, a profit-taking fizzle.

Using Pivots in the Creation of the Nightly Plan

Assume now that you have done your nightly technical analysis, generated a list of potential trade candidates and calculated pivot points for each. Working under the assumption that each pivot line will generate support or resistance, you should be able to quickly determine whether an anticipated move will be sustainable. For example, if your profit target for an intraday trade is one point, but achieving that level of profit requires the successful penetration of two pivot lines, you may want to rethink your strategy. Avoiding a loss often involves limiting profits. In this case, a more reasonable initial target may be the first area of pivot resistance (for long trades) or support (for shorts). Given these levels, if the trade still makes sense from a risk/reward vantage point, keep it on your list. Take profits from a portion of your position when the initial target is reached. Allow the rest of your position to continue moving if the other indicators you rely on as decision support tools indicate that the current trend will continue to move in your favor.

Taking the Trades

When it comes to the trading day, my philosophy is to think as little as possible. I spend a great deal of time putting together my intraday trading plan, and I have found conclusively that I never come out ahead when I second guess the setups during trading hours. The only exception here is the planning of intraday trades that develop in other stocks based on our interpretation of market conditions, and the intraday relative strength of relevant indices. Intraday patterns are covered in Section III.

Setting Stop Losses

I use six types of stops in my trading. The one applied to a trade at any given time depends entirely on what the trade has been doing since entry. This makes the topic pretty subjective, but I think it is worth reviewing.

Intraday Support and Resistance

Setting a stop loss is probably the most important part of creating your nightly plan. Since we only have an educated guess as to what the market will do tomorrow, we need to set our "uncle point" based on price action the day before a trade is to be taken.

I suggest that you use multiple time frames when planning stops. I use a 5 minute chart, since this is what I trade from, and 25-tick and 15 minute charts because they represent higher and lower time frames. The actual stop placement is simply a matter of looking for the peaks and valleys on the intraday chart, and determining where prices tend to cluster. One high does not a stop make. Five or ten, however, and a significant part of the day was spent attempting to move through a price level before failure to push through caused price to move away.

Intraday support and resistance is always my first stop, and combined with the pivot points is how I set the initial profit target. If the distance from the entry to the stop is greater than that from the entry to the projected target, I remove the trade from the plan.

The 8 Period Simple Moving Average (SMA)

Once I have entered a trade, I maintain my original stop until the stock moves to it or moves substantially in my favor. By substantially, I mean at least 50% of the distance to the target. At this point, I use an 8 period SMA to contain the trend, and a violation of .10 below the SMA as a profit protecting stop in a trend.

If price starts to consolidate during the up trend, I use the bottom of the consolidation or the 8 SMA, whichever will keep me in the trade longer. This gives price action room to breathe in the multitude of trendless periods during the day.

Fibonacci Retracement Zones

If price rapidly moves in favor of the trade, intraday support and Resistance and the 8 period SMA will give too much money back to the market for my comfort. When these fortunate situations arise, I use breaks of Fibonacci levels (usually .382 or .618) as exit points. The problem here lies in moves that contain dramatic extensions. In these instances, even the .382 level can be too far away to be practical. For those unfamiliar with the subject, I recommend reading *The New Fibonacci Trader: Tools & Strategies for Trading Success* by Robert Fischer (ISBN 0-471-41910-9) or *Trading with DiNapoli Levels: The Practical Application of Fibonacci Analysis to Investment Markets* by Joe DiNapoli (ISBN 1-891159-04-6) as references on how to use this powerful tool.

Reversal of 2 Closes

When price takes a rapid move in the direction of my trade and then begins to slow down, I watch for a violation of the close of the last 2 bars in the trend for an exit signal. This is a good way to contain a trend that has moved away from the 8 period SMA or does not lend itself easily to a Fibonacci stop. Once again, the caveat is consolidation. When price starts trading in a tight range at the extreme of a move, I use channel boundaries as stops, as a reversal of 2 closes will occur simply as a function of price flipping back and forth in the channel.

The Double Play

This is more of a pattern stop than a stop loss per se. The double play exit triggers when price moves dramatically in our favor in one bar, and then retraces a large portion of that extension in the next. Thus, the bar on the left gives us a large additional profit, while the bar to the right takes much of that profit away. I find that this pattern often indicates exhaustion and a potential reversal. When it occurs, I head for the exit.

The 50% Scratch Stop

Once a position has moved 50% of the distance between my entry and my initial support/resistance target, I move my stop on the trade to just beyond breakeven.

The rules of the game as far as entries and exits go are pretty simple:

1. Enter a trade when the entry price you have planned for ticks. Use a marketable limit order to establish the position. I typically place my buy orders, sell orders, short orders and buy-to-cover orders about .10-.12 beyond the inside quote. This usually results in a fill right around the planned entry price, with the maximum allowable slippage being planned right into the initial order. After that, I do not chase the stock.

2. Set an alert just shy of the stop price and the initial profit target.

3. Sit on your hands and do nothing unless one of your alerts sounds.

4. Exit trades immediately if your predetermined stop price ticks using a marketable limit order

5. When the trade reaches 50% of the distance between the planned entry price and the initial profit target, trail stops just beyond breakeven.

6. When the initial profit target is met, trail stops to intraday areas of support or resistance immediately. If trading large share size, take a portion of the open profit

7. Continue trailing stops as a position moves in your favor. Use intraday support and resistance and/or Fibonacci to establish likely reversal levels.

SUMMARY

The ground rules discussed in this chapter are all about discipline. Developing a disciplined trading methodology is really the only way to get to the point of trading in a non-random, professional manner. Trading is, after all, a business. And no business can survive without a plan.

Section II
The Daily Patterns

CHAPTER 4

Fast Ball

••

... A straight pitch thrown by the pitcher as hard as possible.

When we started our trading career, breakouts on expanded range were so common that all a trader had to do was get up in the morning, buy the continuation move a few pennies above the previous day's high, wait a few minutes and count the money. Unfortunately, those days are over, but breakouts will always be part of trading. The key to capturing profits is in identifying which moves are real, and which will be added to the seemingly endless list of failed patterns. The Fast Ball pattern identifies the breakouts that have all the ingredients to fuel a substantial continuation move, while eliminating most of the trades that would unnecessarily churn an account.

The long trade variety of the Fast Ball pattern works best when the day that completes the pattern comes on the heels of a pullback. Another acceptable variation would be a move that emanates from a consolidation in an uptrend.

The idealized example below illustrates the setup for the long entry. The rules are as follows:

1. The precursor for pattern formation is a pullback in an up trend.

2. The stock must break out of the pullback in the direction of the original trend. The move must represent the widest range of the past ten days, and volume should be higher on the breakout day then the average daily volume during the pullback.

3. On the trigger day, we enter .10 above the high of the breakout bar. Stops should be ratcheted up as soon as the trade is profitable. We close the position by the end of the trading day.

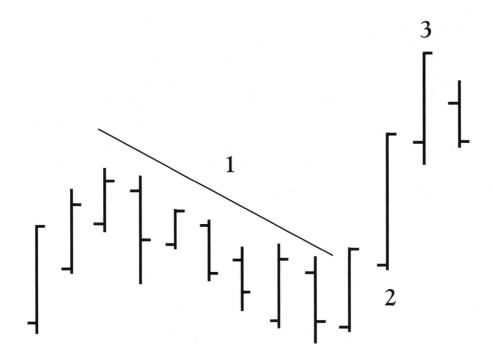

The alternative setup involves a consolidation in a trend, and a range expansion move out of the channel in the direction of the underlying move.

The rules for the long trade are as follows:

1. A trending stock must form a 5 - 15 day consolidation.

2. The stock breaks out of the channel in the direction of the original trend. The move must represent the widest range of the past ten days, and volume should be higher on the breakout day then the average daily volume during the consolidation.

3. On the trigger day, we enter .10 above the high, or .10 below the low (for shorts) of the breakout bar. Stops should be ratcheted up as soon as the trade is profitable. We close the position by the end of the trading day.

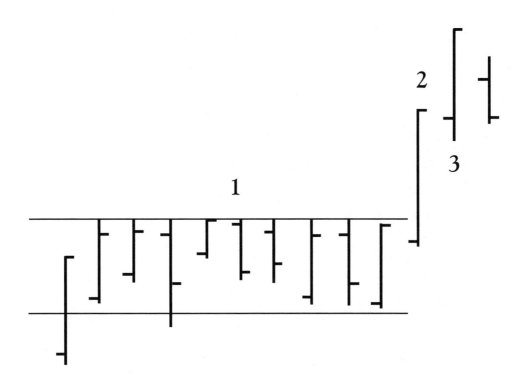

Nike Inc. (NKE) started a climb in September of 2006 that moved the stock in a persistent uptrend throughout the rest of the year. In late October the stock had a pullback to the trendline and a Fast Ball expansion that made for an easy entry with solid follow through.

1.   NKE makes a new high, breaking through resistance that has held the stock for 20 days. The Fast Ball occurs after a shallow pullback in the powerful upward trend.

2.   Entry is immediately after the opening bell at 91.41. The stock traded smoothly higher throughout the session with the deepest intraday pullback being 38.2% of the opening move and a steady climb into a 93.31 close.

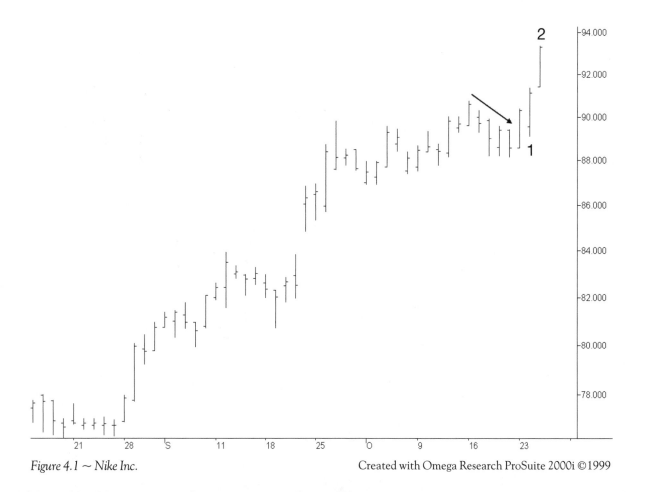

Figure 4.1 ~ Nike Inc.   Created with Omega Research ProSuite 2000i ©1999

While the pullback variation of the pattern is taken only in the direction of the dominant trend, the consolidation type Fast Ball is a trade I will take in either the trend or contratrend direction. This setup often triggers when a stock has consolidated and run out of steam as is illustrated in this example which occurred after Apartment Investment and Management Company (AIV) faltered at all-time highs and started a slide in November of 2006.

1. AIV makes an all-time high and has violent sell-off and a weak close.

2. The stock consolidates in a tight range for nearly two weeks.

3. Sellers push the stock lower in a Fast Ball expansion move that occurs on volume nearly quadruple the AIV average.

4. The short sale is at 54.02, and the stock immediately trades as low as 53.41 before trailing out on a profit-protecting stop. AIV trades higher and triggers a second entry which moves the stock as low as 52.63 prior to a 52.98 trailing exit.

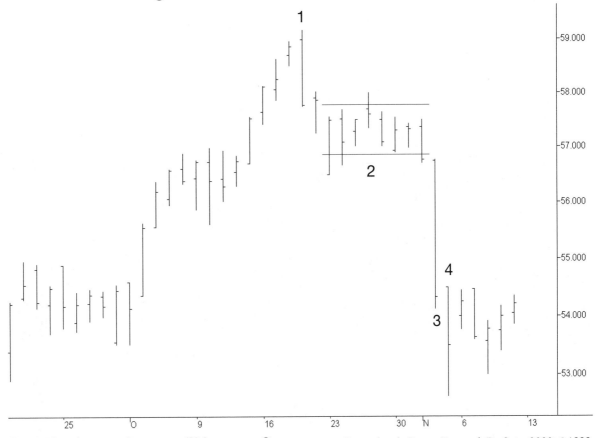

Figure 4.2 ~ Apartment Investment & Management Co   Created with Omega Research ProSuite 2000i ©1999

Energy was as good as gold (better actually) as a trading vehicle in 2006, and coal was no exception. Volatility in basic materials presented many good trading opportunities, and when Peabody Energy (BTU) announced a deal in late November that positioned the company as the provider of most of the coal used in new American plants for the foreseeable future, a Fast Ball move was in the cards.

1. A month-long upward move left a pullback and consolidation on BTU.

2. The Powder River Basin deal is announced, and BTU makes a Fast Ball move higher on nearly double average volume.

3. On the trigger day, the stock adds nearly a point before trailing out on an intraday reversal of two closes exit.

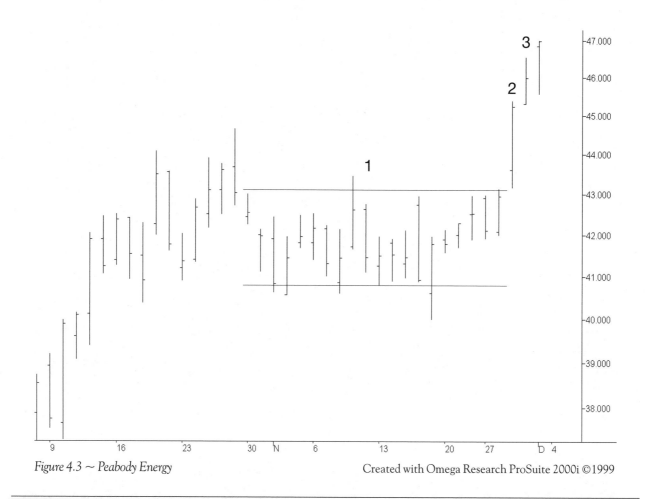

Figure 4.3 ~ Peabody Energy

Created with Omega Research ProSuite 2000i ©1999

Earnings season often leads to solid moves in companies that beat or miss consensus estimates. In a strong environment, any good news can translate into a great move, and when Dow Jones & Company (DJ) announced, for the second time in two months, that advertising revenues were solidly higher, the stock was quick to react with a Fast Ball move.

1. DJ makes a solid move higher on the weekly chart, and has a series of one point multiday moves followed by brief pullbacks.

2. A Fast Ball expansion day as the revenue news is announced.

3. The stock triggers on the opening bell and immediately retraces ¼ point before reversing and booking a profit of .50 per share. After a brief consolidation, the stock continues a trend move that has it up nearly a point going into the close.

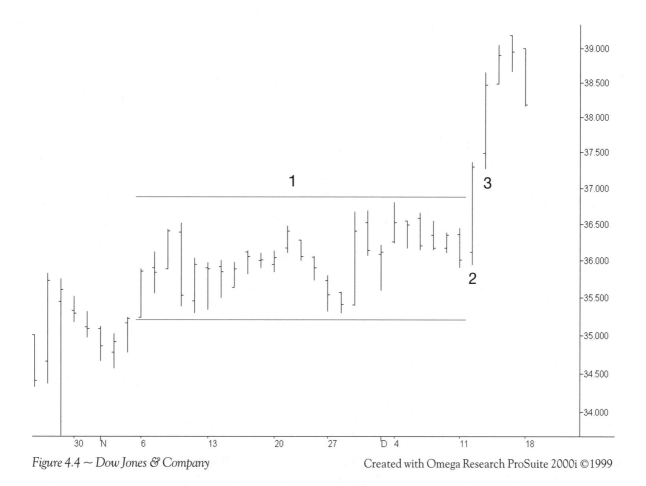

Figure 4.4 ~ Dow Jones & Company   Created with Omega Research ProSuite 2000i ©1999

Overseas Shipholding Group, Inc. (OSG) is a regular on our watch list, as Fast Ball moves in this one occur very frequently. After a steady climb from June through late August of 2006, the stock hit rough waters and made a move lower that wiped out all the constructive price action in under a month. The stock made a few attempts to rally, but ultimately caught another wave lower.

1.   A pullback from recent lows stops short of retracing 50% of the recent decline in OSG. The move culminates in a poor close at approximately the 38.2% retracement level.

2.   A sharp Fast Ball break out of the pullback moves the stock's price solidly below the bottom channel line of the retracement.

3.   The stock opens lower and quickly retraces to the trigger price. By the close, the stock has booked over a point in short side profits.

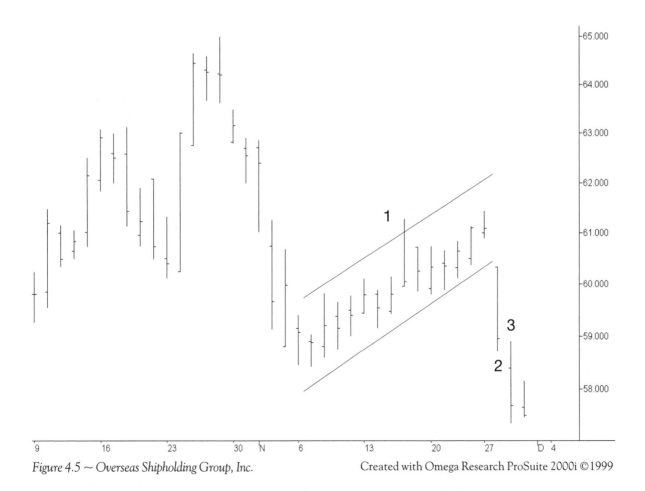

Figure 4.5 ~ Overseas Shipholding Group, Inc.   Created with Omega Research ProSuite 2000i ©1999

Summary

The Fast Ball pattern works because it relies on pent up energy to cause momentum to reassert itself. This makes it a much more conservative approach to trading breakouts than simply entering the continuation of every wide range bar the market hands us. This means that we miss quite a few breakouts to new highs, but with so many range expansions failing, I really don't mind being rained out sometimes. I like this pattern as much for what it avoids as for the opportunities it presents. When the pattern comes together just right, the Fast Ball is a consistent, reliable and conservative approach to riding a quick and profitable move.

CHAPTER 5

Infield Fly

··

… A fly ball with such potential to be caught in the infield that the batter can be declared out immediately upon hitting the ball.

Often times, strongly trending stocks will move too far too fast, making a pullback a foregone conclusion. A reaction open can take a stock much higher than is warranted. The result can be an immediate sell-off or a steady drift back toward the previous day's high. When gap openings are followed by poor intraday price support, the stage is set for a move that will fill the void. Spotting these opportunities and knowing how to capitalize on them is one of the best ways to take money from the market. The key is to find moves in stocks that are showing all the signs of exhaustion. Trading the Infield Fly pattern correctly has proven to be my most predictable and most profitable intraday technique. This is a short only strategy, making for clear, unambiguous entries and exits. The Infield Fly is a bread and butter trade that will test a speculator's short selling skills and provide handsome rewards when follow-through comes our way. While overall market conditions can push the trade toward the desired outcome, a broader move lower it is not necessary for success.

The Infield Fly relies on the fear factor to generate profits. Basically, we are looking for stocks to move sharply to the upside and to be pushed too far in too short a time frame. This setup relies on a gap day to take price higher, and fail to put in a strong close. The next session, we look for a short selling opportunity, and a move to profits.

The entry criteria for the short sale are as follows:

1. A move up on a daily chart culminates with a gap higher which closes in the lower half of its range. Ideally, there is room for profit between the low of the gap day and the high of the previous day, but the pattern works very well even if there is not.

2. The stock must break the low of the gap day by at least .10 to trigger an entry. If the position closes strongly in our favor, we will carry a 30 - 50% portion overnight.

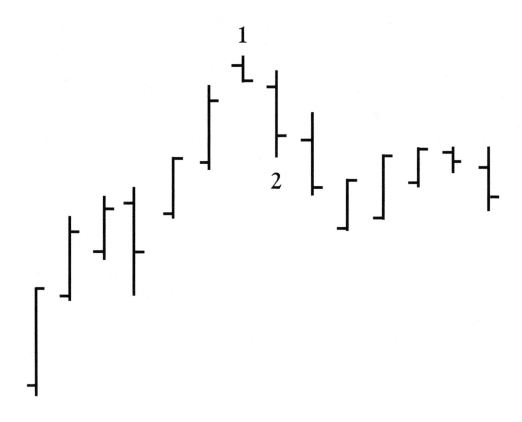

Recent gap attempts can often lend insight into the probable behavior of a stock if it is gapped again. In the case of Autoliv Inc. (ALV) the stock was gapped in mid November, only to retrace lower over the following sessions. When the specialist tried the gap again, we anticipated a good trade and saw the stock make an equally large retracement move in just one session.

1. ALV gaps higher but does not close in the bottom of the range.

2. The stock was off the radar and we miss the retracement move lower.

3. ALV is gapped into the failed price area a second time and closes poorly generating an Infield Fly trading alert.

4. The stock opens and immediately starts selling off. ALV closes back in the range that resolved the first gap move and settles right at three-month support levels.

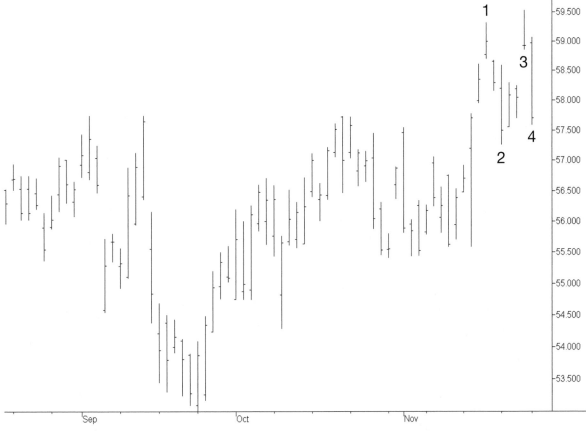

Figure 5.1 ~ Autoliv Inc.

Created with Omega Research ProSuite 2000i ©1999

Franklin Resources, Inc. (BEN) had a solid run in 2006, moving higher from mid-June lows around $80 per share to nearly $115 in November. That gain wiped out earlier 2006 declines and added value that was certain to have profit-takers moving in to collect their gains.

1. After a move higher out of a September/October consolidation range, BEN trades solidly higher and is gapped to an all-time high. The stock trades in a narrow range and closes net positive on the day, but negative on the session.

2. Another attempt to gap BEN higher reverses and takes out the Infield Fly low. The stock trades three points lower by the close and continues the decline into the previous trading range over the next several sessions.

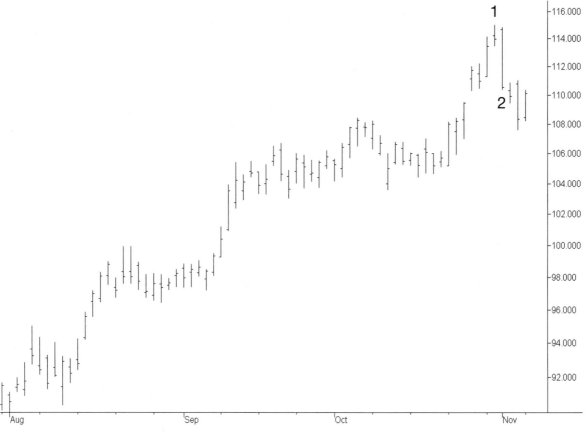

Figure 5.2 ~ Franklin Resources, Inc.   Created with Omega Research ProSuite 2000i ©1999

I trade quite a few retail stocks, and Fortune Brands (FO) is one of the more volatile setups when it presents itself. The stock typically has good intraday moves and fits into the volatility parameters within which I like to trade. When setups occur in this one, they generally have good follow through and nice intra-day travel range.

1. After several attempts to break out of an August congestion range, a gap higher opening has FO above recent resistance. Buyers push the stock, but it is unable to break higher, leaving an Infield Fly setup on the session.

2. The short entry is at 75.04, just below the low of the setup day. During the course of the trading session, FO moves as low as 74.63 before pulling back slightly to close at 74.79, just above the close of the bar that broke out of the congestion area.

3. Over the next several sessions, the stock loses additional ground and makes a last test of the congestion area prices.

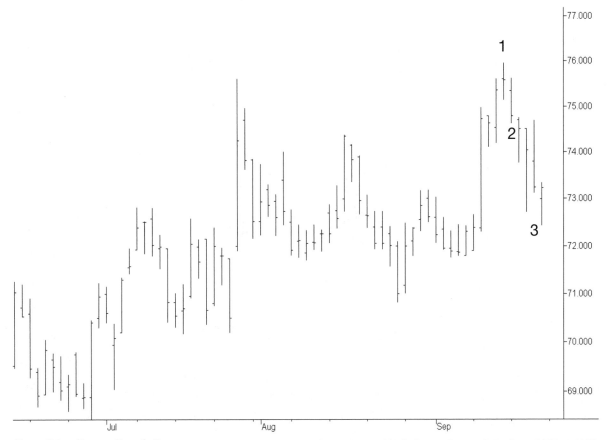

Figure 5.3 ~ Fortune Brands, Inc   Created with Omega Research ProSuite 2000i © 1999

Another retail sector stock I love to keep in my basket is Kohls Corp (KSS). The stock spent much of the past several years on my list of favorite short sale candidates. More recently, the price action has generated setups in both directions. In mid September, however, the stock suffered the same setbacks as other sector favorites, and an Infield Fly just a few days behind a setup in Fortune Brands demonstrates that traders need to stay aware of strength and weakness across all the trading candidates in a group.

1. After sustaining a three year fire sale, KSS makes a long climb on solid price action which culminates in an Infield Fly setup.

2. On the trigger day, KSS gaps higher and begins selling into the setup day lows. The trigger is at 67.32 and the stock trades to a 66.14 low before retracing 40 cents into the close.

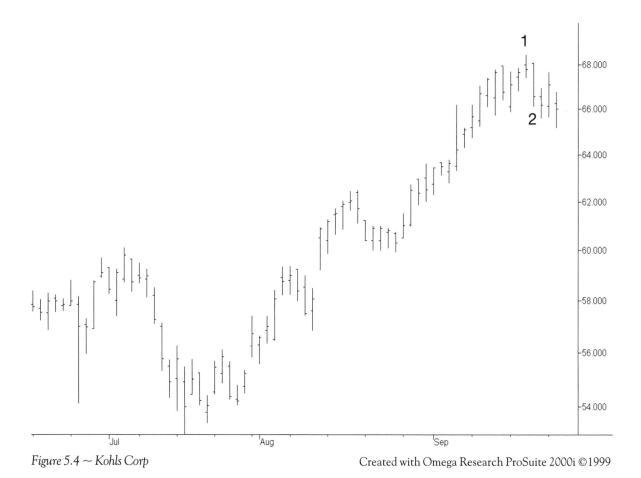

Figure 5.4 ~ Kohls Corp   Created with Omega Research ProSuite 2000i ©1999

Long-time followers of my work know that I am a big fan of the homebuilder stocks. The news-inspired moves are almost constant, and each and every trading week contains at least one economic report that will drive the sector. Lennar Corp (LEN) is one of those stocks that anyone familiar with the sector trades very regularly. And in late 2006 the stock along with its sector brethren fought higher even in the face of almost constant bad new home sales data. That kind of price action always has me on my toes looking for an opportunity to capture some of the bottom-pickers profit taking when it occurs. The Infield Fly is a perfect tool for the occasion.

1. A Fast Ball setup becomes a Backdoor Slider and generates an upside pop. A new wave of buyers comes for LEN.

2. The stock gaps higher and leaves an Infield Fly on the day.

3. LEN makes a one point move in our favor right off the open before closing out on a reversal of two closes profit stop.

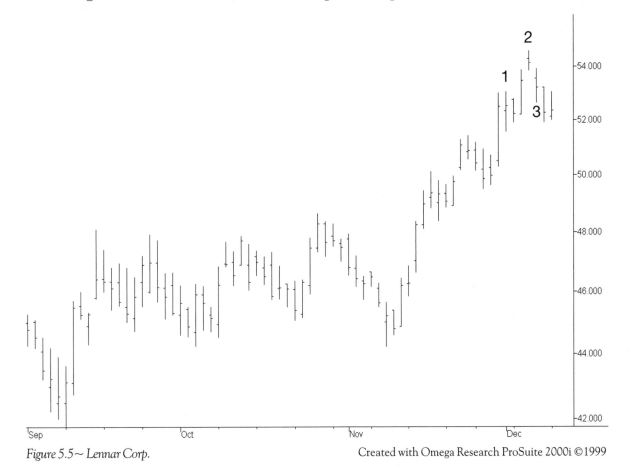

Figure 5.5~ Lennar Corp.   Created with Omega Research ProSuite 2000i ©1999

SUMMARY

Like most things in life, if a stock move looks too good to be true, it probably is. The Infield Fly is a powerful pattern that allows us to capitalize on the irrational exuberance that propelled the stock higher, without having to play the guessing game of picking the top. If the pattern comes in, it usually does so definitively. There is no time to second guess entries, as shorting fast movers can be tricky business. Otherwise, determine the maximum amount of slippage you are willing to accept, and price it into the trade before pulling the trigger. I find that aiming a little lower with these moves provides more opportunity for the specialist to find a fill at an improved price, while lessening the likelihood of the move leaving us behind.

CHAPTER 6

Line Drive

... A ball hit in the air at a low trajectory
directly to a fielder or through the infield.

There is much by way of "common wisdom" regarding reaction moves the day after a breakaway. Many traders avoid any position in the direction of the gap, feeling that price action will be choppy and that there is a virtual certainty that the pattern will fill in over the course of hours or days. Many others will attempt to fade the move in the hope of catching the contra-extension for a profit. The Line Drive pattern seeks to capitalize on those instances in which these individuals are wrong and price continues to advance or decline in the direction of the gap. When this pattern works, it generally hands over quick profits. When it fails, it usually either does not trigger or results in a small loss. These characteristics make it a good intraday trade. I generally close this position at the end of the session. The fact is, most gaps can fill, and the object of the trade is to capture the quick profit, not a continuation move. This is a long pattern trade. I do not use the Line Drive for shorts.

The setup for the long trade is as follows:

1. Today the stock must form a breakaway gap, making a 10 day high. The close must be above the open and in the top 25% of the bar.

2. Tomorrow, we will take a position .10 - .12 cents above the high of the breakaway bar.

3. Trail stops .05 - .10 under intraday support of the breakaway day or .05 - .10 under the trade day Pivot or Support 1.

4. The initial profit target is approximately at the Resistance 1 level.

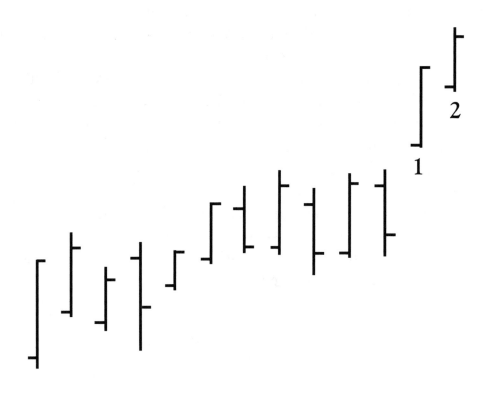

While consensus opinion would stipulate that most gaps fade, reality does not support the assertion. Many gaps happen for good reason, and one good way to separate the follow-through candidates from the fades is with the Line Drive. In this example Abercrombie & Fitch Co (ANF) makes a Line Drive move higher after beating earnings estimates.

1. An event-driven gap propels ANF higher, and the stock has a very strong move throughout the session with a finish at the top of the range.

2. The trigger is early in the session and the trade stays alive for nearly two hours. The exit is on an eight period simple moving average violation.

3. The stock pulls back and begins forming a Switch Hitter setup (see Chapter 9). ANF will stay on our radar throughout the coming sessions, as the strength and follow-through of the gap move are indicative of more potential upside price action.

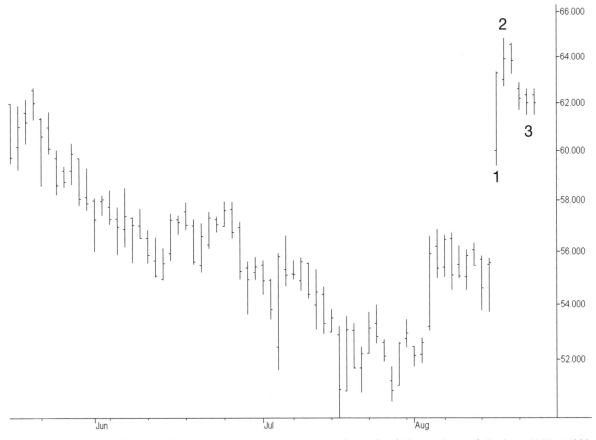

Figure 6.1 ~ Abercrombie & Fitch Co   Created with Omega Research ProSuite 2000i © 1999

Claires Stores Inc (CLE) announced mixed earnings numbers and a lukewarm outlook and immediately started climbing on the news. The stock put in five solid days before making a tradeable Line Drive move, and followed up with a continuation setup which is a pretty typical outcome for the pattern.

1. On the heels of a Fast Ball move and consolidation, CLE puts in a Line Drive day with wide range and a strong close.

2. A long position triggers at 31.60 and the stock makes a move to 32.30 for a solid close.

3. An extension move leads to a retracement and a Switch Hitter setup. Over the next several weeks, the stock continues to trade higher and CLE closes above 33.25 for the year.

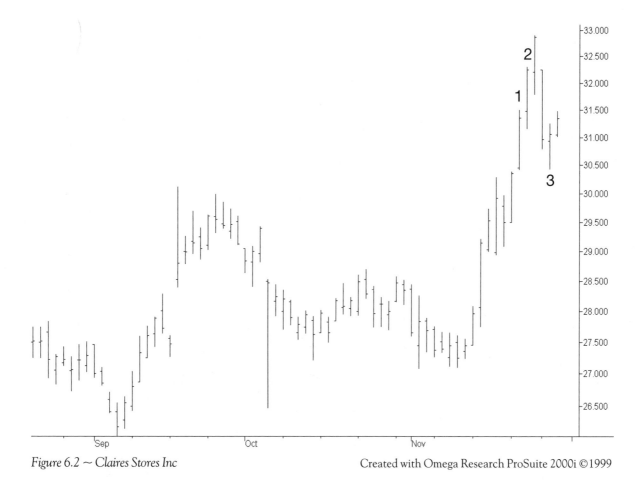

Figure 6.2 ~ Claires Stores Inc   Created with Omega Research ProSuite 2000i ©1999

Line Drive moves tend to follow earnings announcements and preceed larger upside moves. Entergy Corp. (ETR) was expected to report strong results in October 2006, and managed to beat the street's estimates in terms of earnings per share and revenues. The news set the stock in motion, and the ensuing Line Drive momentum pushed the stock to new highs through the end of the 2006.

1.   ETR gets earnings related momentum and puts in a Line Drive move with all the characteristics I like to see in a long side candidate. The stock gapped higher, held the gap, traded smoothly throughout the session and put in a strong close in the top of the intraday range.

2.   The stock triggers right off the open and has a three-quarter point climb before multiple profit stops trigger an exit of a portion of the position. ETR continues climbing into the end of the year, and swing traders have the opportunity to add a solid ten percent gain to the position.

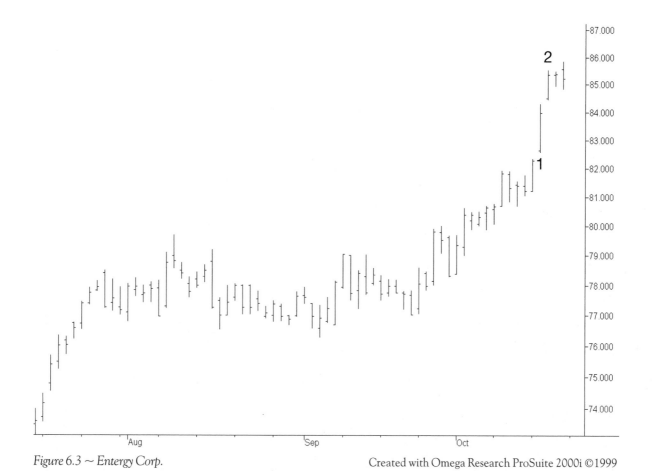

Figure 6.3 ~ Entergy Corp.   Created with Omega Research ProSuite 2000i ©1999

Overseas Shipholding Group Inc (OSG) is another regular trade for us. In this example, the stock made its move in anticipation of a pending earnings announcement and in the absence of any significant news. Intraday price action on the setup day becomes important in assessing the potential of the setup.

1.   OSG makes a Line Drive move. The range on the day is not particularly wide, but the gap day puts the stock back above the failed breakout range of a few days earlier. Also, the intraday price movement of the stock is consistent with the price expansion continuing. The stock makes repeated moves higher followed by periods of consolidation on the 5-minute chart, and buyers exert steady pressure throughout the session.

2.   On the trigger day, OSG opens and moves down to intraday support. A smooth move up to the trigger price results in an entry and a solid one-point move into the close with almost no intraday bleedback.

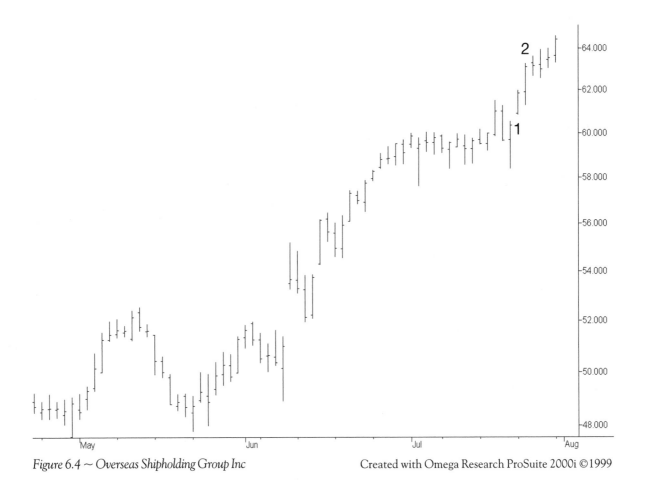

Figure 6.4 ~ Overseas Shipholding Group Inc   Created with Omega Research ProSuite 2000i © 1999

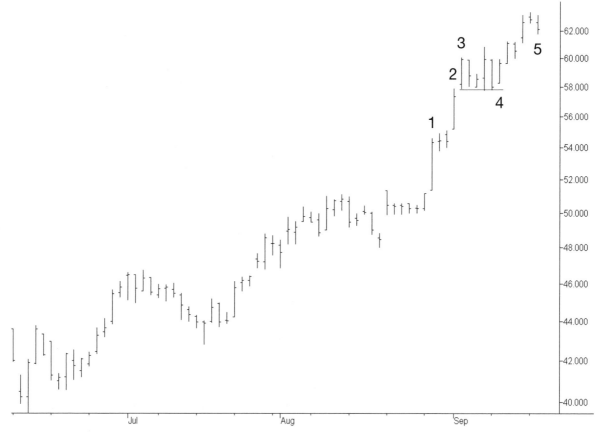

Vimpel-Communications (VIP) is a good example of why traders need to continually reevaluate what a stock might be up to. When multiple signals start to present in the same direction, a stock will often provide many opportunities to profit in both the shorter and longer term.

1.   VIP makes a Fast Ball move higher out of a consolidation range. The pattern develops into a Backdoor Slider setup.

2.   VIP triggers the Backdoor Slider and closes deep in profits, leaving a Line Drive with good range and a strong close on solid intraday price action.

3.   The stock opens higher and backfills slightly. The trigger is in the first five minutes of trading, and by 9:45, VIP has a point in open profits. By 10:15, another point is added to the move.

4.   An area of daily support develops and presents a logical stop for any swing position in VIP.

5.   Two weeks after the Line Drive, the stock is trading $6 higher.

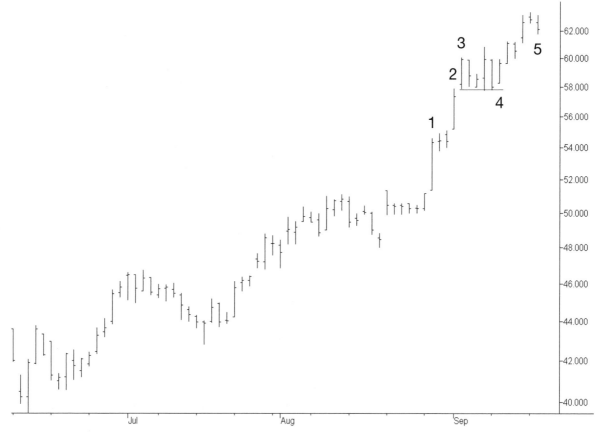

Figure 6.5 ~ Vimpel-Communications ADR   Created with Omega Research ProSuite 2000i ©1999

SUMMARY

The Line Drive is a simple pattern that works well when a stock, the underlying sector and the market are trending. It capitalizes on the ability of a security to gap open and hold its gains without immediately filling the void between the current session low and the previous day's trading range. Given the volatile nature of the current markets, I use this pattern strictly as a day trade but if we see a strong upward trend exert itself, then the Line Drive can set up some nice swing positions.

CHAPTER 7

3-2 Pitch

....

... A make-or-break pitch that determines
if the batter will hit, walk, or strike out.

Make-or-break setups don't come along that often, and when they do, they are rarely worth the effort involved in finding them. The 3-2 Pitch is an exception to the rule. This one takes days to form, and many potential setups never trigger. When a 3-2 Pitch does trigger an entry, it can make for a profitable intraday or swing trade with a good risk/reward ratio. The pattern relies on market participants to push a trending stock rapidly higher and then sell it off for profits. Then, when all the gains of the upward thrust seem to be in danger of turning into losses, the strong money enters the market and jettisons the stock higher again. When the move plays out, we hold a portion overnight as a swing trade.

Often, traders drive price higher on good volume and with an expanded trading range. These are the ingredients that create the Fast Ball setup. Unfortunately for breakout traders, profits must often be taken quickly on these moves as they are much more prone to failure than they were in the bull market of the 1990's. The 3-2 Pitch pattern uses a Fast Ball failure and a subsequent pullback as the primary ingredients for a long setup that can lead to substantial profits.

Here are the rules for buys (short sales are reversed):

1. A Fast Ball break.

2. The trigger either does not happen, or results in a loss.

3. The stock has a 1 - 5 day pullback.

4. We enter on an intraday breakout of the high of the deepest pullback bar.

5. A portion of any profitable position is carried over as a swing trade.

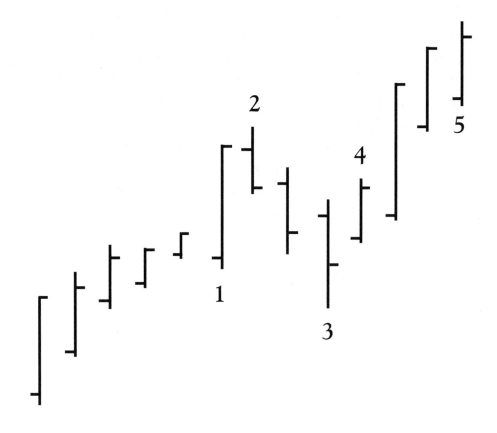

On April 21, 2006 Arch Coal, Inc. (ACI) reported revenues of $634 million vs. consensus of $560 million and full-year earnings per share of .84 cents against estimates of .57 cents. That proved to be just what investors wanted to hear, as the stock was off to the races with the buyers scrambling to get shares.

1. ACI makes a Fast Ball move higher the Monday after the earnings gap. The close is in the top quarter of the bar, but not as strong as might be expected given that Credit Suisse, Merrill Lynch and Morgan Stanley upgraded the stock prior to the open with targets over $100 per share.

2. The stock has a four-day pullback, with a low in Switch Hitter retracement territory, giving us even more confidence in the potential of the setup.

3. ACI triggers and moves more than two-points in our favor.

4. Over the next eight sessions, the stock adds another $4 per share.

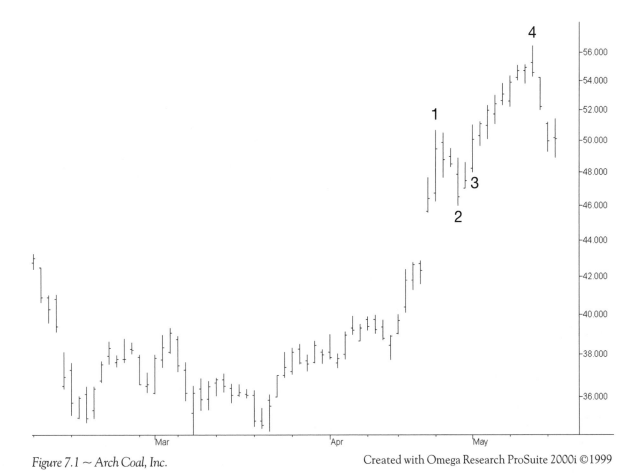

Figure 7.1 ~ Arch Coal, Inc.   Created with Omega Research ProSuite 2000i ©1999

Becton Dickinson & Co (BDX) illustrates an important point. Traders need to think like traders. Opportunities are found on both sides of the market, and it is important not to hold a bias as to where a stock is headed.

1.   BDX makes a Fast Ball move higher out of a consolidation range.

2.   Following a shallow pullback, the stock has a 3-2 Pitch trigger day with a constructive close above the Fast Ball high.

3.   The stock makes a three-point move over eight trading sessions and leaves an Infield Fly setup which triggers the following session.

4.   Another Fast Ball setup. BDX closes in the middle of the range.

5.   The stock completes a 3-2 Pitch / Switch Hitter multiple-signal pullback and triggers another short entry.

6.   The low of the move represents another two-point profit.

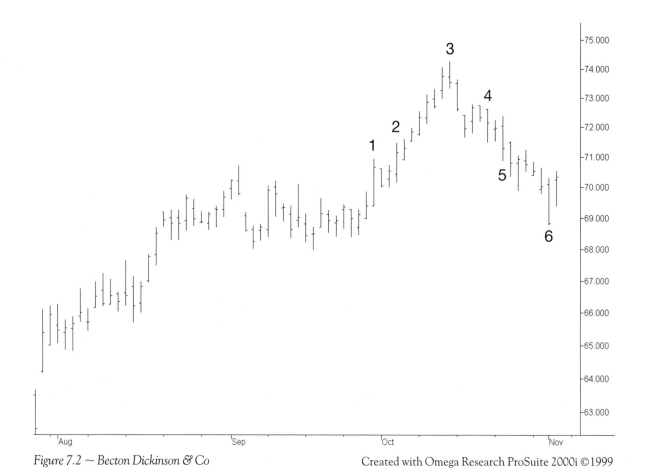

Figure 7.2 ~ Becton Dickinson & Co   Created with Omega Research ProSuite 2000i ©1999

Oil and Gas stocks provide plenty of volatility for the active trader to capitalize on. Those who watched anything oil related in 2006 know that this was definitely the hot sector in terms of intraday moves. Conoco Phillips (COP) is a stock that should be on every trader's daily watch list.

1. After a test of interim support, COP accelerates its move lower with a Fast Ball expansion which closes with a bounce.

2. The stock makes a three-day 3-2 Pitch move higher.

3. The trigger day generates a two-point profit on the short position.

4. By the time the stock finds support, another two points are added to the position's profitability.

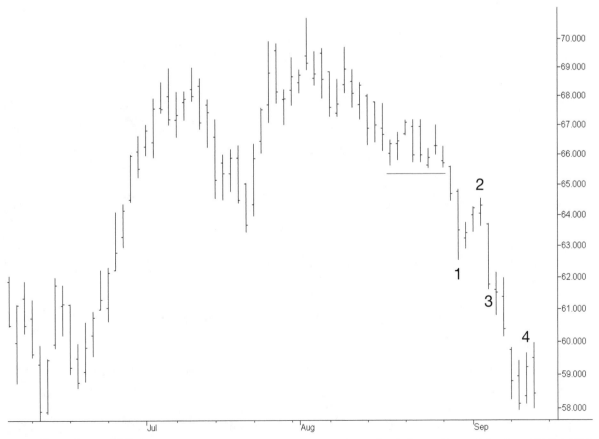

Figure 7.3 ~ Conoco Phillips   Created with Omega Research ProSuite 2000i ©1999

Additional 3-2 Pitch signals over the swing holding period are a sign that things will continue to move in the right direction and also provide an opportunity to add to the position.

1. Quest Diagnostics Incorporated (DGX) has a gap higher and makes a Fast Ball expansion. The stock consolidates its gains in the middle of the trading range.

2. The 3-2 Pitch pullback triggers a long entry.

3. Another Fast Ball is followed by a shallow 3-2 Pitch setup. The stock maintains its persistent uptrend.

4. A Fast Ball pop out of a short consolidation is followed by another 3-2 Pitch that pulls in to the top of the consolidation range.

5. An exhaustion close more than $4 from the original entry.

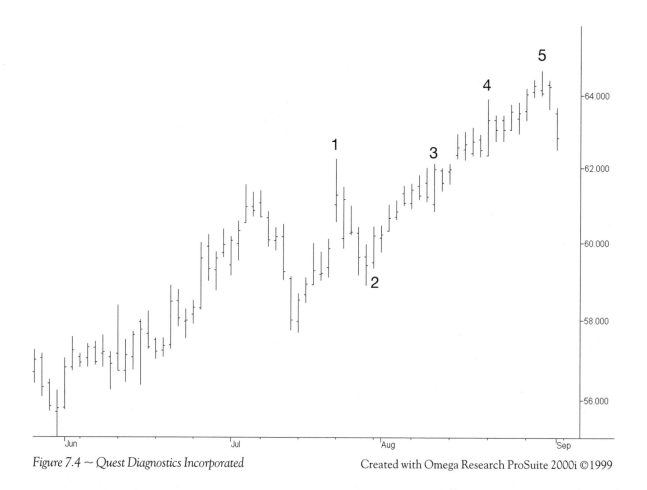

Figure 7.4 ~ Quest Diagnostics Incorporated Created with Omega Research ProSuite 2000i ©1999

Late 2006 had many of us speculating about a potential bottom in the housing market. Whenever traders start talking about the home builders, I have five favorites that are immediately on the radar. Toll Brothers Inc (TOL) is one of those stocks.

1. TOL has moved off its lows in several waves of solid price action. The stock makes a Fast Ball move higher and hits weekly support. A 3-2 Pitch retracement begins.

2. The stock breaks above the high of the lowest bar in the pullback and triggers a 30.71 entry. The close has the position up approximately $0.30 per share. The intraday high was just above October/November resistance.

3. The stock trades as high as 33.57 as economic data are released that put the likelihood of an interest rate reduction in doubt.

Figure 7.5 ~ Toll Brothers Inc   Created with Omega Research ProSuite 2000i ©1999

SUMMARY

The 3-2 Pitch is an important setup for two reasons. First, it provides good intraday stability and profit potential when it triggers. I think this is because of the variety of market factors that are required for its formation. Second, it keeps us in a portion of the trade for what can often be a much larger move. This can contribute handsomely to long-term profitability and survival as a trader. The key to trading this pattern is patience. There will be many false setups that continue to drift lower once they begin pulling back. This will be particularly true in downward-trending markets. When everything falls in place, however, the 3-2 Pitch makes for very good trading.

CHAPTER 8

Backdoor Slider

....

... a pitch that appears to be out of the strike zone,
but then breaks over the plate.

Patterns usually don't play out exactly the way we expect them to. Part of the job of a trader is to adapt to what is really happening instead of swinging at what we think is coming over the plate. Every breakout trader eagerly anticipates the range expansion as a move with great potential for a drive right over the fences. Many of us stop looking at these setups when they fail to immediately follow through, leaving a great potential setup behind in the process. This pattern provides a second or third-day entry that can be more reliable then trading the anticipated follow-through day.

The basic premise here is that when range expansions occur, the market often needs time to digest the gains or losses. If the next trading day consists of a consolidation with an extreme close in the same direction as the expansion, a lucrative opportunity exists for a continuation move one or two days later.

The logic of the pattern is very easy to follow. We are basically looking for a Fast Ball setup to fail to break out. We then want to see the momentum of the move cause directional energy to consolidate near the range extreme. Within a few days, we look for entry as the pattern breaks in the direction of the momentum.

The example below illustrates the setup for the long entry. The short entry works equally well, and is just the reverse. The rules are as follows:

1.   On day one, a Fast Ball pattern sets up.

2.   On day two, or as many as three additional days, the stock should make a narrow range day, failing to substantially break the day one high. The additional days in the pattern should close in the top quarter of the Fast Ball day range.

3.   On the trigger day, entry is .10 above the high of the Fast Ball day.

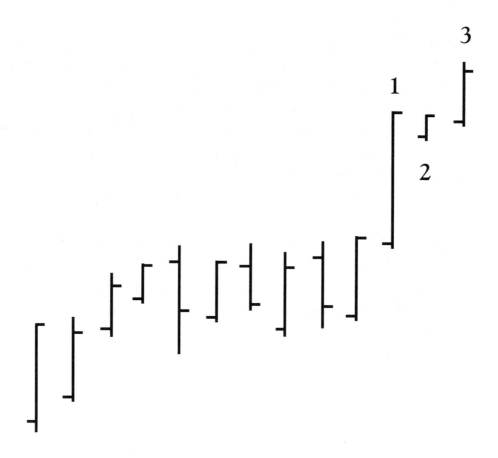

Retailers are frequently in play. Earnings announcements, ICSC-UBS store sales, Redbook chain store sales, and the large number of consumer indices reported every week make for some good trading among the members of the group. When things really get going, Best Buy Co. (BBY) is almost always at the top of the list of trading opportunities.

1. BBY reports second quarter revenue and same store sales. The numbers are better than consensus forecasts, and the stock has a Fast Ball expansion of range and volume.

2. The stock forms a Backdoor Slider on the daily chart, with two inside days consolidating in the top of the Fast Ball range.

3. Entry is at 52.74, and the stock makes a 1.25 point move in the first hour of trading.

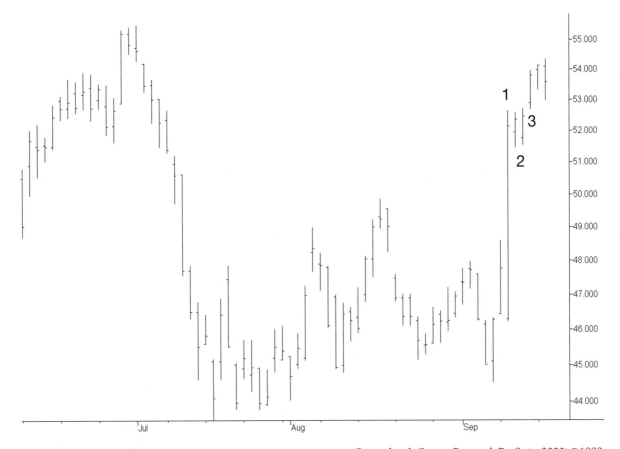

Figure 8.1 ~ Best Buy Co. Inc.   Created with Omega Research ProSuite 2000i ©1999

The gains being consolidated when a Fast Ball expansion leads to a Backdoor Slider have the potential to generate further violent moves in the direction of the trend. However, the move that starts the pattern does not have to be extraordinary. It just has to meet the requirements of a Fast Ball setup. I judge continuation potential as a function of how well the stock manages to maintain price action in the top of the Fast Ball bar during the consolidation.

1. Centex Corporation (CTX) has a Fast Ball move higher, and two days of Backdoor Slider consolidation with closes in the top of the Fast Ball range.

2. The stock triggers an entry at 56.33 on the first five-minute bar of the day. CTX finds support right around the entry price fifteen minutes into trading. Over the next hour, the stock trades .90 higher before retracing and stopping out at 56.80 on a reversal of two five-minute closes.

3. The following session provides a 58.42 Extra Innings (see Chapter 10) entry and extension.

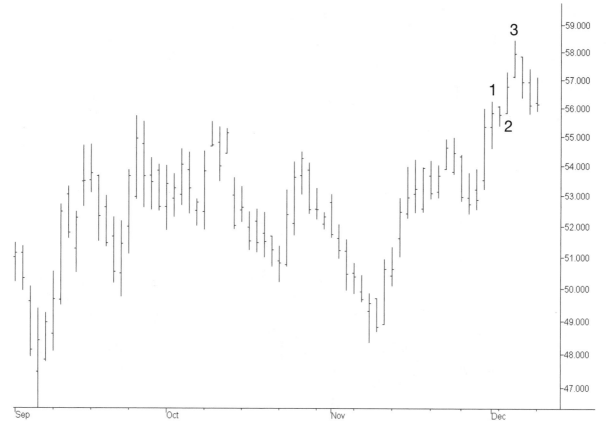

Figure 8.2 ~ Centex Corporation   Created with Omega Research ProSuite 2000i ©1999

Merrill Lynch & Co. (MER) lost nearly 20 points between April and June of 2006. When the company announced that it would submit a plan to improve its Japan operations, selling climaxed and the stock started moving higher.

1. We have a Fast Ball day and a strong close as the stock moves off its recent bottom. The stock consolidates gains the following day, forming a Backdoor Slider that trades in the top 50% of the Fast Ball bar.

2. The Backdoor Slider entry triggers at 70.30 and books better than a one-point gain over the course of three hours.

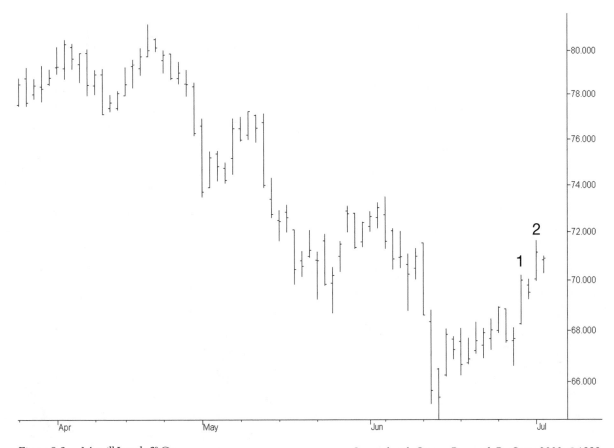

Figure 8.3 ~ Merrill Lynch & Co.   Created with Omega Research ProSuite 2000i ©1999

A long trading range had McGraw-Hill Companies Inc (MHP) consolidating gains in a monthly uptrend in late summer and early fall of 2006. The street was expecting the company to beat consensus estimates, and when the numbers were in, earnings were indeed better than expected, but revenues were a bit light.

1.   MHP reports third quarter results, and the stock moves out of a three-month trading range in a Fast Ball expansion of range and volume. The stock consolidates gains on the second day of the setup, creating a Backdoor Slider entry opportunity.

2.   A 63.29 print triggers the entry, and MHP moves to 64.42 during the first hour of trading. The trade closes out on a profit stop at 64.25 after the stock violates the 5-minute 8-period simple moving average and reverses two closes in the intraday trend.

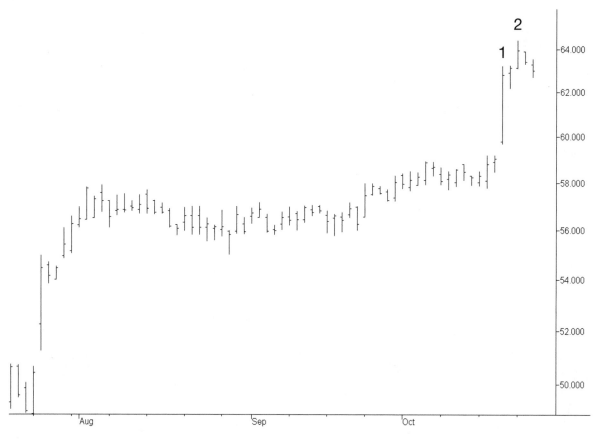

Figure 8.4 ~ Mc Graw-Hill Companies Inc   Created with Omega Research ProSuite 2000i © 1999

Universal Corp. (UVV) nicely illustrates the ability of multiple signals to compound profits over several days while keeping risk manageable.

1.   UVV makes a Fast Ball expansion of range and volume. A follow-through attempt generates a small profit and closes in Backdoor Slider territory.

2.   We are in the right place at the right time, as the Backdoor Slider gives way to another Fast Ball setup and a significant gain on the session.

3.   The Fast Ball setup triggers and makes a two-point move on the session. Another Fast Ball setup is left on the day, and the following session produces a Backdoor Slider.

4.   The Backdoor slider entry triggers and generates another one-point intra-day move.

5.   Over the next several sessions, Extra Innings entries trigger more trades. The entire series generates six points per share, all with no overnight risk.

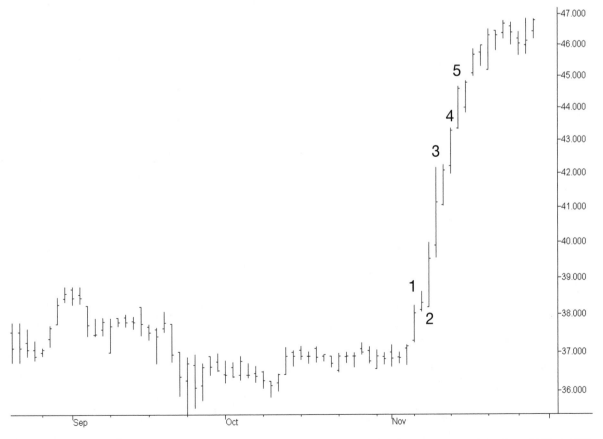

Figure 8.5 ~ Universal Corp   Created with Omega Research ProSuite 2000i ©1999

SUMMARY

Markets almost never do what we expect them to. Substantial price thrusts set the stage for additional profits, but often a few consolidation days are required for rapid advances or declines to lead to additional extensions. The Backdoor Slider pattern gets us into the market at the right time by anticipating these two or three-day consolidations and waiting to trigger a trade until follow-through is present.

CHAPTER 9

Switch-Hitter

■■

*… A player who is able to bat right or left handed, generally
from the opposite side from which the pitcher throws.*

Strong directional moves are usually followed either by consolidation periods or pullbacks in the direction of the dominant trend. Although many traders advocate entering breakouts of these retracements the moment a higher tick is in place, better opportunities are to be had when some specific criteria are met. The Switch-Hitter pattern focuses particular attention on the characteristics of the most extreme day of the move in an attempt to filter out pullbacks that lack the potential for follow-through. In doing so, many potential trend reversals are eliminated before they have a chance to cause losses.

The Switch-Hitter is a pullback pattern that establishes a position after profit-taking has caused a one-to-five day correction in a trend. Several filters are used to differentiate the Switch-Hitter from moves with less profit potential.

First, the magnitude of the initial up or down wave should represent a minimum of 5% (10% for stocks priced under $40 per share) of the value of the equity being traded. This is important since the largest initial profit target we normally expect over several sessions in a pullback entry is a move back to the 100% extension of the initial wave. If we are trading a $30 stock that makes a move up to $33 and enter on a 50% pullback, our logical profit objective is 1.5 points. A 38.2% retracement would yield a target of approximately 1.15 points.

Now assume that our time frame has been shortened, and we wish to take only an intraday position. While this reduces our risk, it also substantially tightens the profit objective. Logically planning the initial profit target for an intraday trade may only yield a move from the 50% retracement back to the 38.2% level established earlier in the correction. Thus, a 10% upward swing in a $30 stock yields a move of 3 points. A 50% retracement moves the stock down 1.5 points. Now, an intraday entry with an initial profit target around the earlier 38.2% level will yield approximately .36 points on the trade. An initial move representing less than 10% of the value of the stock would not be worth the trouble or the risk in entering the position.

The second criterion I look for during the pullback is decreasing volume. Buying or selling pressure should always be greatest when price is moving in the direction of the 20-period SMA. If the volume during the corrective wave approaches that of the initial wave, then the trade has a lower probability of success than it does when volume increases as price moves in the direction of the underlying trend.

Third, I always examine the relative strength of the stock as reported in *Investor's Business Daily* prior to planning the trade. This trading strategy essentially seeks to buy strong stocks, or short weak ones, when they are compressed and ready to release some energy. Long side candidates should have a minimum relative strength rating of 60. Conversely, short sale setups should present relative strength readings of 30 or less.

The final step in picking the good setups is to examine the price behavior of the most strongly correlated underlying sector. Thus, if I am considering a trade in Anglogold Limited (AU), I would look at the Philadelphia Stock Exchange's Gold & Silver Index (XAU.X) to determine whether or not AU is behaving erratically compared to its index.

All that being said, the ideal long setup looks like the chart below. The rules for shorts are reversed.

1.   A first move ends with a two-week high.

2.   A correction takes price down as low as the 61.8% retracement and closes above its opening price, and preferably in the upper 25% of its range.

3.   We open a position on trade above the high of the retracement low bar.

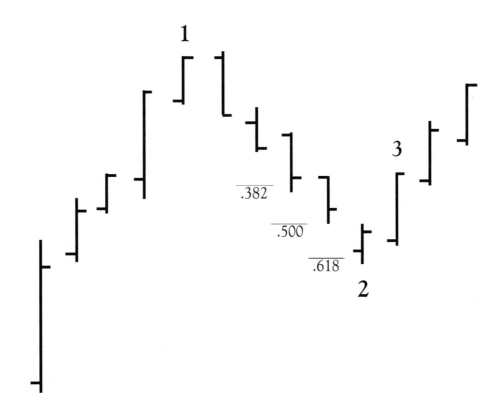

When the retail sector starts trending, the regular stocks on our watch list are a good place to look for multiple trend-following signals and trades that allow for much of a move to be captured with maximum risk management.

1. Abercrombie & Fitch Co. (ANF) makes a Line Drive move higher. The stock triggers on the bar marked B and has a nice intraday profit.

2. The A – B – C swing is a 38.2% Switch Hitter retracement which initiates a 61.90 entry. The initial target is at the point B high.

3. The C – D – E swing is a 61.8% Switch Hitter retracement which initiates a 64.77 entry. The initial target at the point D high is quickly surpassed and is the trailing stop on the balance of the open position.

4. The E – F – G swing is a 38.2% Switch Hitter retracement which initiates a 69.53 entry. The initial target is at the point F high.

5. A Fast Ball setup which triggers the following session for an intraday profit.

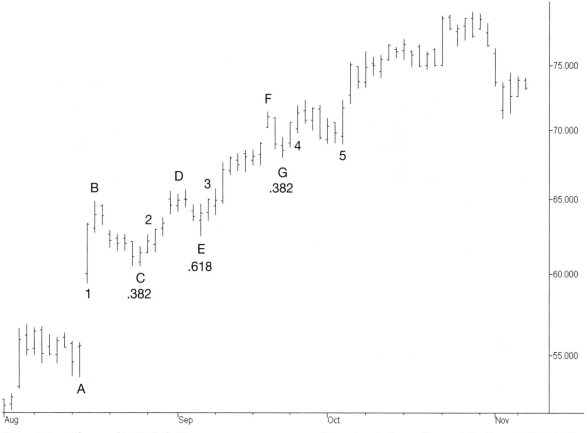

Figure 9.1 ~ Abercrombie & Fitch Co   Created with Omega Research ProSuite 2000i ©1999

The volatile auto parts sector is another good place to find strong setups in retail stocks. Autozone Inc. (AZO) provides many trading opportunities, often making extended moves with very symmetrical characteristics.

1. AZO triggers a Switch Hitter buy of the A – B – C 50% swing move. The initial target is at point B and is surpassed when the entry day bar makes a Fast Ball move on the session.

2. The upward move culminates with a C – D – E 38.2% Switch Hitter pull-back and entry. The entry bar forms a Line Drive setup and easily clears the initial target at point D.

3. An E – F – G swing and Switch Hitter entry on a breakout of the .382 pull-back. Once again, the initial target at point F becomes the trailing stop.

4. The G – H – I move is a 50% Switch Hitter retracement. The entry takes a position that trends steadily to almost $115 per share.

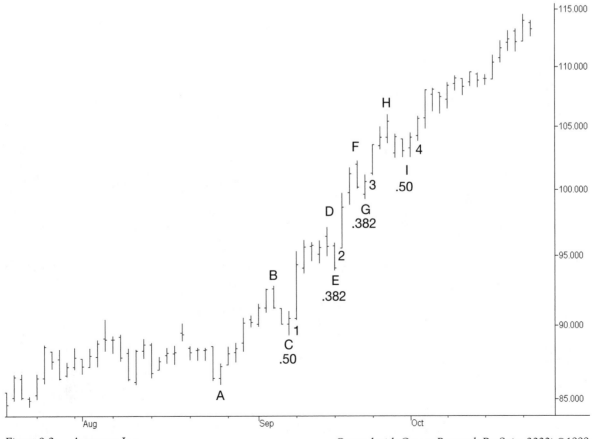

Figure 9.2 ~ Autozone Inc   Created with Omega Research ProSuite 2000i ©1999

Oil stocks can make some pretty violent moves. 2006 was definitely a tank half full — tank half empty kind of year, as oil and gasoline prices had wild swings on supply and geopolitical news. Conoco Phillips (COP) was a stock in the sector that frequently made it to my list of daily setups.

1.   The stock triggers a short sale after the A – B – C swing move. Point C represents a 38.2% Switch Hitter retracement of the A – B move. When the market opens on September 6, 2006, COP immediately starts printing red. However, the stock is a Regulation SHO pilot list security, so it can be shorted on a downtick making for an easy fill.

2.   The stock makes a five-day extension of the Switch Hitter move, and closes out on a daily violation of closing prices.

Figure 9.3 ~ Conoco Phillips   Created with Omega Research ProSuite 2000i ©1999

Prudential Financial Inc. (PRU) mirrors the Insurance Sector Index (IUX.X) very closely. The stock is both technically and fundamentally one of the most attractive in the insurance group, and can act as a sector leader, providing clues as to the coming behavior of other related stocks.

1. PRU has completed an A – B – C swing move, with the C low representing a 50% retracement of the A – B leg. This represents the first good pullback since the stock started its upward move in early September. The underlying sector, IUX.X, has just put in the same ratio move over the same time frame. The entry leads to a quick upside move, with the initial multiday target at point B.

2. The initial target is achieved, and PRU pushes higher in a Fast Ball expansion of range and volume. This is a good time to tighten trailing stops.

3. After another leg higher, PRU trails off in a sideways consolidation.

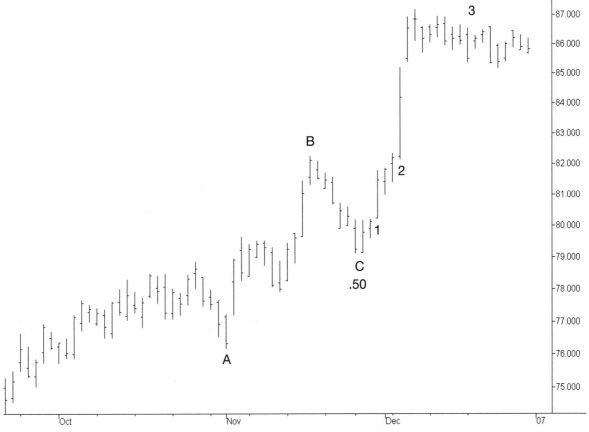

Figure 9.4 ~ Prudential Financial Inc   Created with Omega Research ProSuite 2000i ©1999

Regency Realty Corp (REG) is a midcap REIT that typically trades very low volume. With the caveat in mind, the stock is really only of interest when the REIT's are in play and trending. Low volume stocks can make for nice swing profits, but the first sign of congestion usually has me looking for the door. Indecision in a thin stock can lead to trouble as reversals can be fast and violent.

1.   REG puts in a Fast Ball expansion of range and volume.

2.   On the Fast Ball trigger day, the stock makes a solid trend move.

3.   An A – B – C swing move sets up the 75.91 Switch Hitter entry. The C point low is a 38.2% retracement of the A – B move. The stock closes the session with a one-point profit.

4.   After an 80.04 profit protecting exit a few sessions earlier, REG makes a C – D – E swing move and triggers a Switch Hitter long entry that stops out on a violation of the stop designated by the line above point E.

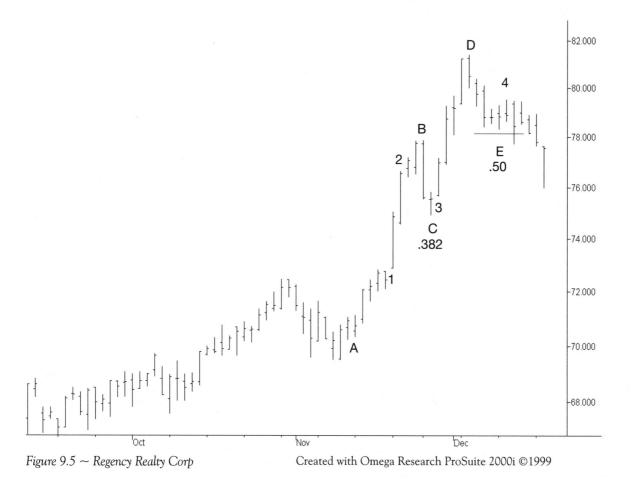

Figure 9.5 ~ Regency Realty Corp   Created with Omega Research ProSuite 2000i ©1999

SUMMARY

If used with the proper discretion, pullbacks can yield solid gains. The key is recognizing entries that represent pauses in the strongest moves. The Switch-Hitter takes a classic chart pattern and redefines it to make it stronger. Although the criteria limit the number of potential entries, the quality of the trades generated more than compensates for the reduction in their frequency. As intraday and swing techniques go, this one can yield impressive results. This is especially true when traders take the time to validate the underlying trend and make certain that sector correlations support the entry.

CHAPTER 10

Double Header

....

… Two games played back to back by the same teams.

Nothing lasts forever. The best teams can suddenly drop game after game to their seemingly inferior rivals. And even the worst clubs turn around and win a few. Double Headers are daily reversal patterns that have the potential to generate good profits in the course of undoing recent price action. Although the greatest potential for this setup is when it occurs as the last gasp in a pullback during an established trend, it also works well as a means of spotting and capitalizing on the end of a move.

Charts are made up of large numbers of short waves that together form a longer-term trend. At the peak or valley of each of the short-term moves, we often times find the Double Header pattern signaling that a low or high has been put in. When this happens, a low risk entry is presented, offering the alert trader the opportunity for intraday and multi-day profits. The pattern is easy to spot, and generally pretty simple to trade.

The long and short trade setups are shown in the chart below.

1.   Price moves to a low. Trading in the following session creates a near mirror image of the first day's move. Both bars should open and close near the extremes of their range. When both bars are in place, the first criterion of the setup is met.

2.   The long entry is .10 - .15 above the high of the reversal bar. The profit target is A, the high of the bar on the day immediately preceding the setup.

3.   Price trends to an interim high. We wait until the reversal bar is in place, and the two bars together create the Double Header confirmation.

4.   The entry is .10 - .15 below the low of the reversal bar. The profit target is B, the low of the bar on the day immediately preceding the setup.

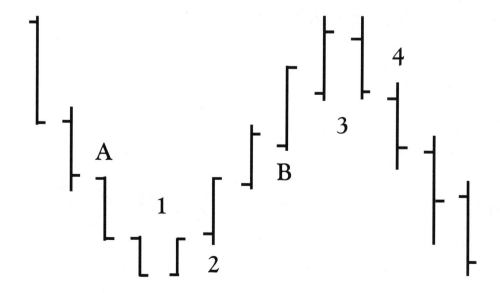

Industrial gas provider Air Products & Chemicals Inc (APD), trades around a million shares per day, and has an average true range of approximately $1, giving it both the liquidity and volatility necessary to make for some good trades.

1. A strong move to the downside and we have a Double Header setup.

2. The pattern entry is at 61.36, the high of the reversal day bar. The trade moves through the profit target (A) for the intraday trade.

3. APD tries to break back into the May – June trading range and forms another Double Header setup.

4. The stock makes a .80 move, reverses for a profit stop and triggers a second entry generating an additional 1.20 in profits.

5. A rally is stopped by July resistance and forms another Double Header.

6. An entry trigger produces a fractional gain on the session.

Figure 10.1 ~ Air Products & Chemicals Inc   Created with Omega Research ProSuite 2000i ©1999

Oil and Gas sector plays are some of the most volatile positions a trader can hold. News and earnings push these stocks around far more than most of their non-energy counterparts, and Cameron International Corp. (CAM) is no exception.

1.　　The stock is gapped lower a week prior to its second quarter earnings announcement. The street widely expects CAM to meet or beat consensus. A Double Header setup forms, indicating a potential move into earnings.

2.　　The stock hits the trigger price and quickly trades to the initial profit target. A reversal triggered a profit-protecting stop, only to have the stock trigger again and make a large range move into the close.

3.　　Over the next two days, CAM extends its gains. On the day of the earnings announcement, a gap open has the stock up five points from the entry price a few days earlier.

Figure 10.2 ~ Cameron Intl Corp　　　　　　Created with Omega Research ProSuite 2000i ©1999

General Dynamics (GD) has a propensity for good moves and disturbing intraday volatility. When the defense stocks are gyrating, I will take a position in this one with reduced share size to alleviate the stress associated with hard swings.

1. A sharp reaction move rockets off a recent bottom and pushes the stock into a Double Header setup.

2   The trigger day gaps right into the entry price. Although this does nothing to quiet the morning abdominal butterflies, the trade winds up in the plus column with a .70 cent gain on the session.

3. Another reaction move creates another setup.

4. The Double Header triggers and yields over a point on the session.

5. Another attempt to break higher generates a third setup.

6. GD triggers a short sale and generates another decent intraday profit.

Figure 10.3 ~ General Dynamics Corp   Created with Omega Research ProSuite 2000i ©1999

Prior to releasing third quarter results, Monsanto Co. (MON) shares showed signs of a slump. Evidently, the good people at Merrill Lynch did not feel the agri-chemical producer deserved the downside price action, as the brokerage released a statement indicating that the reduced price presented a golden buying opportunity. The result was a textbook setup.

1. A move lower on earnings jitters finds support on the brokerage recommendation. Moves prior to earnings reports tend to be overreactions, so the setup is definitely interesting to traders looking for a move.

2. With earnings a day off, the stock appears to be in fertile ground as the entry triggers and MON closes more than 1.25 points above the entry price. In my experience, holding stocks over into the announcement has never been a good habit to get in to, and MON is no exception. Insiders are known for buying the rumor (or starting it) and selling the news, so the risk reward is seldom justified.

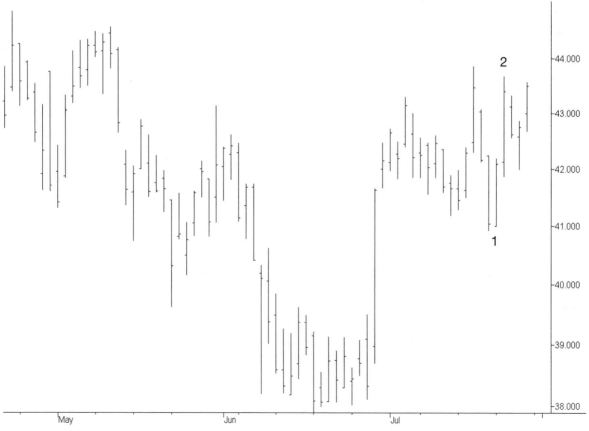

Figure 10.4 ~ Monsanto Co.   Created with Omega Research ProSuite 2000i ©1999

Many Double Header setups are a reaction, or overreaction to news events. Some-times, however a stock moves in the absence of such an event, reflecting volatility in the broader markets. Waste Management Inc. (WMI) made just such a move in late-December 2006.

1. WMI sells off with the broader market as traders digest economic news and proselytize the overbought nature of the markets. The concern is short lived, and the market and WMI rebound, forming a Double Header in the stock and in the Dow Industrials.

2. The entry triggers at 36.52 and generates better than a half-point move over the course of the session.

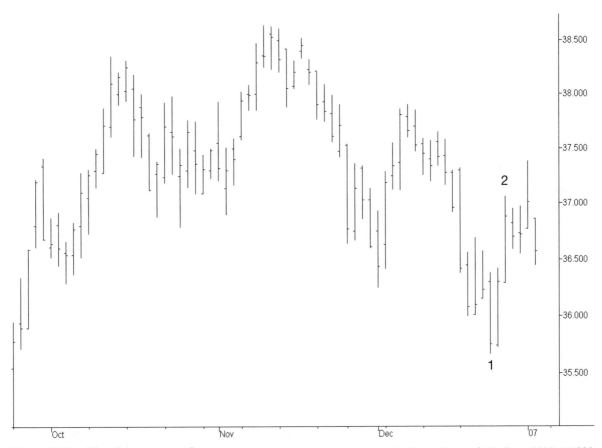

Figure 10.5 ~ Waste Management, Inc.   Created with Omega Research ProSuite 2000i ©1999

SUMMARY

The Double Header provides an excellent means of identifying reversal moves as they are forming, rather than attempting to jump on board in the days that follow. When it triggers, it is generally easy to catch, and when it fails, the Double Header tends not to get us in at all. The pattern does not present as frequently as some of the others discussed here, but when it does, I find it reliable and, best of all, profitable. The parameters of the setup are a little trickier to program for computer scanning than some, but chart flipping for these is relatively easy because of the distinctive appearance of the setup.

SECTION III
THE INTRADAY PATTERNS

CHAPTER 11

Extra Innings

··

… Occasionally the outcome of a game cannot be decided during the course of nine innings. In these situations, extra innings determine the ultimate winner.

The best trading plans often turn into piles of scrap paper when nothing hits on trigger day. Sometimes though, opportunity knocks twice and a great trade emerges late from a plan that seemingly failed us. I call these situations Extra Innings. They demonstrate the ability of vigilance and focus on the details of trading to generate profits.

Capitalizing On The No Hitter

I am including my Extra Innings strategy to focus on the fact that the business of equities trading requires flexibility. Extra Innings is actually an extension of each of the daily patterns, but since it requires intraday monitoring and strategizing, it is included in this section. Days on which few or no trades trigger could easily be called No Hitters and forgotten about. What I do instead is take the setups that did not blow out against the plan, and save them for the next day or two.

Much of what we do requires the cooperation of the market. My plans are almost always for continuation entries in the direction indicated by a stock's fundamentals, relative strength and multiple time-frame trend. If we plan for an entry on a break outside a tight consolidation range, and there is no trigger, that plan does not become invalid. The stock simply took a breather. The only reason I would eliminate a non-trigger from the radar is if a move completely contra to the trend and the planned entry occurred. If it looks like a reversal, it's usually a good idea to back off.

Most of the setups in *Around the Horn* lend themselves to Extra Innings entries. A Backdoor Slider is, of course, a variety of the Fast Ball in Extra Innings. The Backdoor Slider, Infield Fly, the Line Drive, the 3-2 Pitch, and the Switch Hitter all provide very good second day entry opportunities. Again, the distinction between Extra Innings and a pattern failure is that the latter occurs when there has been a violation of the setup day criteria. We never look to enter a pattern failure continuation. We only take the Extra Innings entry when the stock has done nothing wrong. It simply took a day or two to pause.

In this chapter, I will show you some actual Extra Innings triggers that occurred in 2007 based on patterns that were identified for the previous day in my Intraday Trading Service. Remember as you examine each one, we are looking for the spirit of the setup to remain unaffected by the previous day's failure to trigger.

Extra Innings is an almost sure fire way to add profits to your bottom line. I strongly suggest that you add this simple strategy to your trading arsenal.

The Backdoor Slider is a great pattern to trade. When it sets up as described in Chapter 8, it is both easy to conceptualize and very logical in terms of execution levels and position management. When the Fast Ball energy yields to the consolidation of the Backdoor Slider, pent up energy is what sets the follow-through trade in motion. We generally are looking for the momentum to reassert itself within one or two days. Sometimes, the market can be a little more indecisive. In those circumstances, extended Backdoor Sliders can make for fantastic Extra Inning game winners.

1. A Fast Ball setup gets 2007 off to a good start for Autozone Inc (AZO).

2. The Backdoor Slider setup does not trigger within my normal scanning parameters, but we keep the stock on the radar looking for some post-holiday buying. The fade back into the Fast Ball range (A) does not invalidate the setup, as the close is back in the consolidation area.

3. AZO triggers and yields almost two points in profits.

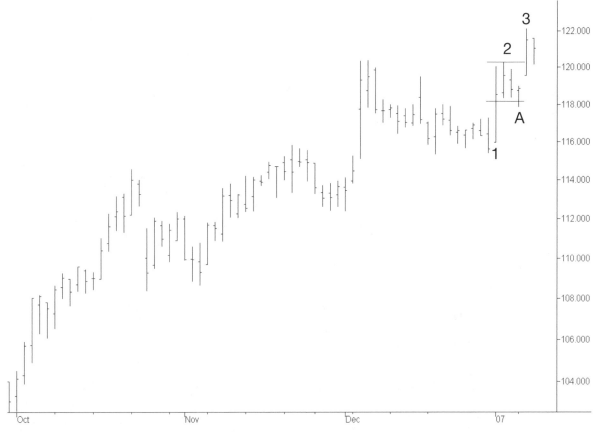

Figure 11.1 ~ Autozone Inc.   Created with Omega Research ProSuite 2000i ©1999

Expanding volatility during the consolidation days of a Backdoor Slider usually negates the setup, as the pent up energy we are looking for dissipates prior to a continuation move. However, when I see a strong underlying trend favoring the momentum of the Fast Ball move, I will keep an Extra Inning Backdoor Slider on the radar for a few sessions to explore the possibility of additional momentum.

1. An upwardly trending, triangle formation on the Cemex (CX) daily chart is followed by a Fast Ball expansion and a broadening consolidation pattern.

2. Buying pressure returns and the stock makes an Extra Innings move higher, breaking the consolidation range upper boundary and adding $0.50 per share on the session.

Figure 11.2 ~ Cemex S.A.B. de C.V.　　　　　　Created with Omega Research ProSuite 2000i ©1999

Following the market and knowing the personalities of individual stocks are ground rules no trader can afford to forget. In mid-January 2007, earnings season was in full swing, and Stryker Corporation (SYK) was due to report after the closing bell on January 25. The stock had been building momentum over the past two weeks and the earnings release proved to be a profitable Extra Innings setup for traders who knew to keep the stock on screen.

1.   The Fast Ball entry is identified and we plan a 59.10 entry for the next day.

2.   The stock triggers the entry price and makes a move higher. A quick reversal at the 50%-to-target area signals an exit for a scratch stop.

3.   A Backdoor Slider forms, but breaks up over the next several sessions.

4.   The stock is on the watch list on January 26, 2007, as the previous night's earnings announcement is better than expected. By the end of the session, SYK is trading $1.40 above the Extra Innings entry price.

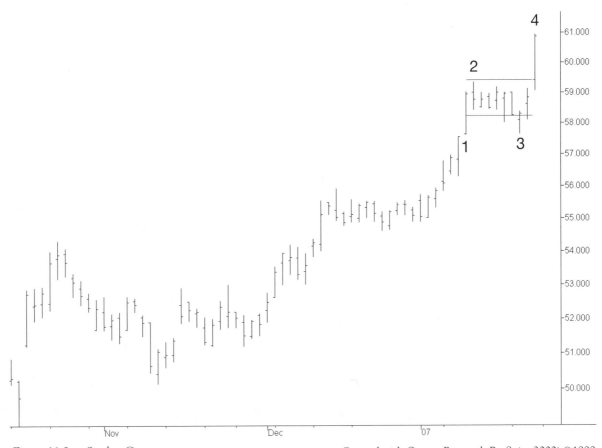

Figure 11.3 ~ Stryker Corp.   Created with Omega Research ProSuite 2000i ©1999

Switch Hitter setups are most attractive when they have a sharp peak and valley formation. That implies one or two bars at the high and low and smooth trading between them. The Extra Inning of this pattern simply involves a longer, less pointed stay at one of the extremes of the move or retracement.

1.	Cigna Corporation (CI) forms a 38.2% Switch Hitter retracement of the extended run A-C and a 50% retracement of the B-C move. The stock consolidates for most of the week (D), but stays on the watch list as an Extra Innings setup. It has not violated the lower boundary of the retracement zone and is simply in a congestion range.

2.	An entry trigger as CI trades higher by over $1 on the session.

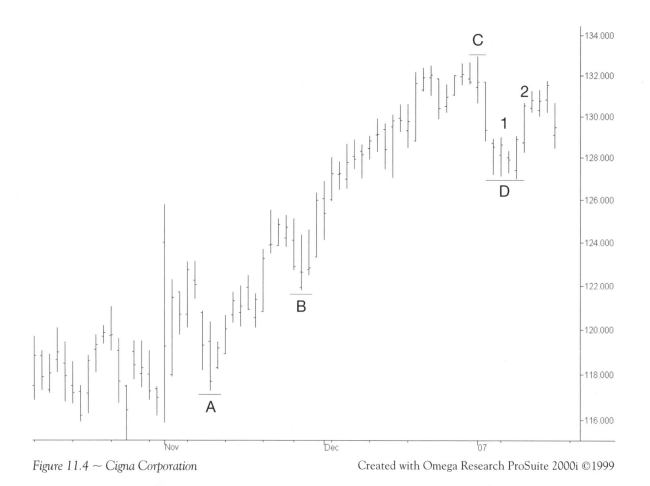

Figure 11.4 ~ Cigna Corporation		Created with Omega Research ProSuite 2000i ©1999

When a stock generates multiple signals in the same direction over the course of a few weeks, I become hyper-vigilant in the search for Extra Innings setups.

1. RenaissanceRe Holdings, Ltd. (RNR) has an Infield Fly day leading to a successful trade and a close in the middle of the range.

2. A Double Header setup leaves another bearish signal on the daily chart.

3. The pattern fails to trigger an entry, and leaves a daily Extra Inning.

4. A short sale below the Double Header low generates nearly $1 in profits over the course of the session and leaves a daily Fast Ball setup.

5. The initial Fast Ball entry generated a scratch stop, but the stock formed an Extra Inning in a downward sloping consolidation range.

6. RNR triggers a short sale at 58.25 and closes the day with $0.85 in profits.

7. Over the next two sessions, RNR moves as low as 55.11 before retracing.

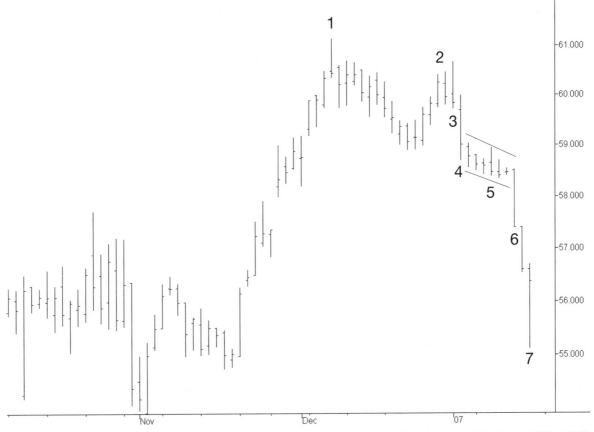

Figure 11.5 ~ RenaissanceRe Holdings, Ltd   Created with Omega Research ProSuite 2000i ©1999

SUMMARY

The Extra Innings entries emphasize that as traders, we must have the courage and conviction to follow our plan through to its logical conclusion. Sometimes things don't go as per the playbook. That does not mean that it is time to sell the team or fire the coach. Rather, we need to be willing to look for opportunity when it is located in the most obscure of all places — right in front of us.

CHAPTER 12

Baltimore Chop

....

*… A ground ball that hits in front of home plate (or off of it)
and takes a large hop over the infielder's head.*

Trading the open can make for a very rough ride. Things can get particularly hairy when there is a significant gap due to erratic behavior in the overnight futures markets. The Baltimore Chop is an intraday pattern that uses basic statistics and five-minute bars to find a high probability turning point after an overreaction opening. It is easiest to execute as a long strategy from a sharp gap down open, but it works equally well as a short sale. The only caveat is that, if there are a lot of traders shorting the move, we sometimes have trouble getting quick fills.

The Baltimore Chop relies on some basic principles of statistics to derive a setup. For those of you who shudder at the very thought of mathematics, take a deep breath and rest assured that it's going to be all right, because the concepts that need to be understood are the most fundamental computations in any first year college text on the subject. That being said, there are three inputs that are required to compute the parameters for trade entry. The first is the Standard Deviation (SD). The formula is as follows:

$$SD = \sqrt{average\ of\ (deviations\ from\ average)^2}$$

In this case, the average we are using in the calculation of SD is the mean value of True Range which represents price volatility by calculating the difference between the True Range High and the True Range Low. To perform the calculation for each day in a series, note the current bar's high or the previous close, whichever is greater. Call that value TRH. Next, note the current low or the previous close, whichever is lower. Call this value TRL. Now perform the simple calculation TRH - TRL and voilà, True Range!

Now comes the fun part. We will walk through the process of performing the calculations for validating the Baltimore Chop pattern. Once this portion of the chapter is completed, you should be able to enter the formulas into your real-time charting software and obtain alerts when any of the stocks on your scan list meet the criterion established.

Let's use some actual recent data to perform the calculation. The time period is October 9 - October 20, 2006. The market was trending strongly, with minor S&P resistance right around the 1370 level. Gap openings occurred regularly, and movement in the S&P 500 futures acted like a magnet to pull the gap down openings up and the gap up openings down. This made for a good trading environment, with the dominant trend being a good predictor of follow-through and contratrend opportunities also present if we were to looking for them.

The stock we will examine in the example is Encore Acquisition Co. (EAC). The true range values have already been calculated and are as follows:

Encore Acquisition Co. NYSE : EAC	
10/09/2006	0.75
10/10/2006	0.85
10/11/2006	0.79
10/12/2006	1.00
10/13/2006	0.38
10/16/2006	0.68
10/17/2006	1.05
10/18/2006	0.57
10/19/2006	0.91
10/20/2006	0.77

Table 12.0.1 ~ EAC Daily True Range Data

Now, we solve for SD by finding the square root of the average of the deviations for the ten true range cases we are examining as follows:

$$SD = \sqrt{\frac{\sum\left(X_{1-10} - \overline{X}\right)^2}{10}}$$

which yields:

$$SD = \sqrt{\frac{0.397}{10}} = .1994$$

The equation yields one standard deviation from the mean. Adding SD to the average and then adding it to the high (high + (SD+average)) and subtracting it from the low (low-(SD+average)) accounts for 68% of the variability we would normally expect in either direction of price movement. For the purposes of the Baltimore Chop entry, we are interested in two standard deviations, which accounts for 95% of the expected range of price. To accomplish this, we simply double the standard deviation. Next add the doubled standard deviation to the mean. The result, 1.17 is now again added to the high and subtracted from the low price of the stock. The resulting prices are the levels at which we will look to fade a gap the following morning. Then, we have the following:

Lower Gap Reversal Zone   24.87 - 1.17 = 23.70

Upper Gap Reversal Zone   25.64 + 1.17 = 26.81

Table 12.0.2 shows the summary statistics for Encore Acquisition Co. for the days considered here. These are easily derived, necessary to complete the gap computations and tell us a great deal about what is going on with the stock. Most analytical software will provide these descriptives, and it is always good practice to display them for the core group of stocks that you will be trading.

This completes the process of calculating the Gap Reversal Zones for the Baltimore Chop pattern. Next, we will look at the rules for pattern entry. Then we will examine the actual move in Encore Acquisition.

Descriptive Statistics	
Mean	0.78
Standard Error	0.06
Median	0.78
Standard Deviation	0.19
Sample Variance	0.04
Range	0.67

Table 12.0.2 ~ Encore Acquisition Co.

Once the calculations for the setup are mastered and programmed, this a pretty simple pattern to find and trade. To make it work, you need to establish a means of finding morning gaps in either direction, establish 2.0 SD validity and then monitor for volume and price to indicate a reversal is in the making.

The ground rules are as follows:

1. A gap opening sends price dramatically away from yesterday's close.

2. An interim support/resistance area forms at or beyond 2.0 standard deviations above the high, or below the low, of yesterday's range and the market fails to confirm the extension by way of volume.

3. We enter the trade just above the high (long trade) or below the low (short trade) of the last bar in the pullback. If the stock trades in a consolidation range before reversing, we enter on a breakout of the range.

4. The profit stop is maintained at the reversal of 2 closes on a 5-minute chart, or at a 38.2% retracement of a larger move.

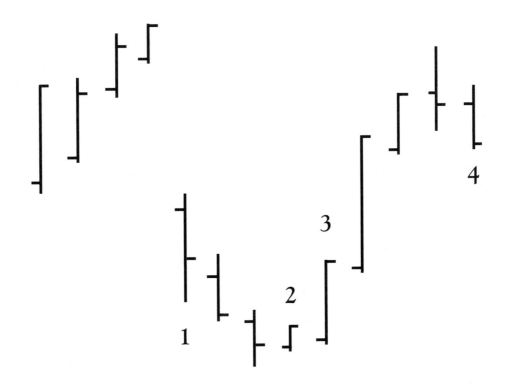

On October 22, 2006, Encore Acquisition Co. (EAC) revised its production guidance lower by about 1,000 barrels of oil equivalent per day. As is the case with such announcements, the market did not appreciate the bad news, and a gap was in the cards for the following session. As we saw earlier, the stock would have to gap to 23.70 or lower in order to make a 2SD move in the morning. EAC did just that and more, with an opening plunge that wiped out constructive price action that had occurred earlier in the month, leaving the stock perched just above recent lows.

1. An opening drive lower on negative production news and EAC immediately finds buyers.

2. Entry is at 23.58, just above the high of the lowest bar in the pattern.

3. The buyers push the stock as high as 24.45 before a reversal of 2 closes stops the trade at 24.35.

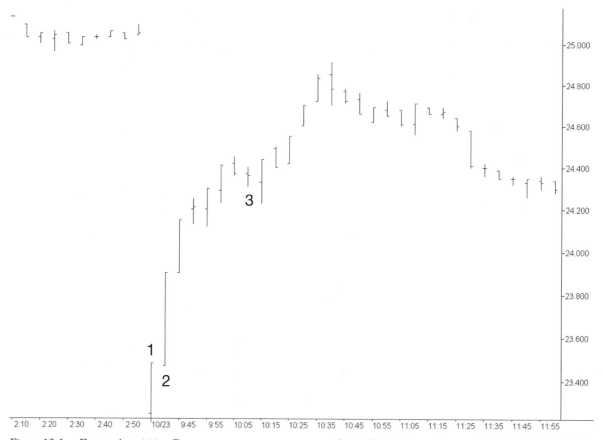

Figure 12.1 ~ Encore Acquisition Co.   Created with Omega Research ProSuite 2000i ©1999

Encore Acquisition Co. NYSE : EAC	
10/09/2006	0.75
10/10/2006	0.85
10/11/2006	0.79
10/12/2006	1.00
10/13/2006	0.38
10/16/2006	0.68
10/17/2006	1.05
10/18/2006	0.57
10/19/2006	0.91
10/20/2006	0.77

Table 12.1.1 ~ 10 Day EAC TR Values

Descriptive Statistics	
Mean	0.78
Standard Error	0.06
Median	0.78
Mode	
Standard Deviation	0.20
Sample Variance	0.04
Kurtosis	0.46
Skewness	-0.63
Range	0.67
Minimum	0.38
Maximum	1.05
Sum	7.75
Count	10.00
Confidence Level (95%)	0.14

Table 12.1.2 ~ EAC Summary Statistics

Precision Cast Parts (PCP) reported second quarter revenue of $1.32 billion vs. consensus estimates of $1.27 billion before the October 24, 2006, bell and the stock was off to the races with an opening gap larger than 2SD.

1. The stock opened beyond the 2SD threshold and immediately dropped by ½ point.

2. The stock made a quick move lower, triggering an entry, before showing strength and starting a move to the high of the morning.

3. PCP breaks through the stop loss just above the high of the session. The second entry trigger is raised to the low of the third 5-minute bar, the highest low in the pullback.

4. A second entry is triggered at the low of the first 15 minutes of trading.

5. Profits are taken intra-bar as the stock reverses two closes.

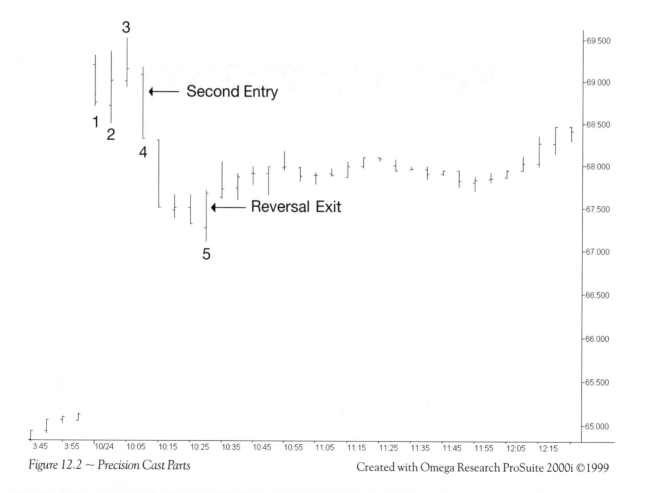

Figure 12.2 ~ Precision Cast Parts

Created with Omega Research ProSuite 2000i ©1999

Precision Cast Parts NYSE : PCP	
10/10/2006	0.80
10/11/2006	1.70
10/12/2006	2.79
10/13/2006	0.84
10/16/2006	1.53
10/17/2006	2.24
10/18/2006	1.48
10/19/2006	1.37
10/20/2006	1.72
10/23/2006	0.99

Table 12.2.1 ~ 10 Day PCP TR Values

Descriptive Statistics	
Mean	1.55
Standard Error	0.20
Median	1.51
Mode	
Standard Deviation	0.62
Sample Variance	0.39
Kurtosis	0.45
Skewness	0.76
Range	1.99
Minimum	0.80
Maximum	2.79
Sum	15.46
Count	10.00
Confidence Level (95%)	0.45

Table 12.2.2 ~ PCP Summary Statistics

Station Casinos Inc. (STN) is a stock on our frequent flyer program. This example is a 2SD gap down following third quarter revenue of $346 million vs. consensus estimates of $351.9 million.

1. The stock gaps lower and immediately starts to find buyers.

2. STN triggers and trades higher by over $1.

3. A reversal of 2 closes triggers an exit.

4. Second entry is triggered over the high of the lowest bar in the pullback.

5. Another exit is triggered on a reversal of two closes, yielding a total of over a point on the two trades.

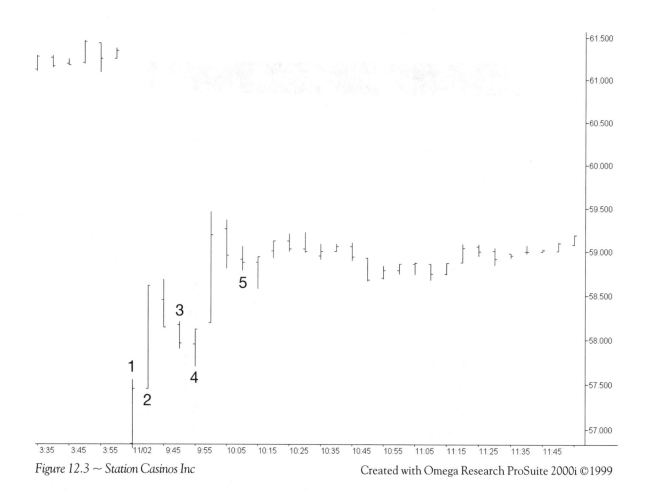

Figure 12.3 ~ Station Casinos Inc   Created with Omega Research ProSuite 2000i ©1999

Station Casinos NYSE : STN	
10/19/2006	1.66
10/20/2006	1.39
10/23/2006	1.29
10/24/2006	1.38
10/25/2006	1.25
10/26/2006	2.90
10/27/2006	1.67
10/30/2006	1.81
10/31/2006	1.32
11/01/2006	1.61

Table 12.3.1 ~ 10 Day STN TR Values

Descriptive Statistics	
Mean	1.63
Standard Error	0.15
Median	1.50
Mode	
Standard Deviation	0.49
Sample Variance	0.24
Kurtosis	6.11
Skewness	2.32
Range	1.65
Minimum	1.25
Maximum	2.90
Sum	16.28
Count	10.00
Confidence Level (95%)	0.35

Table 12.3.2 ~ STN Summary Statistics

On November 16, 2006 wire services reported Investor Carl Icahn and New York real-estate company Macklowe Properties offering shareholders of Reckson Associates Realty (RA) a 9% premium over a previous deal offered by SL Green Realty Corp. The result was a Baltimore Chop opening move that had plenty of room for profits.

1.   A 2SD pop on the open and a close in the bottom of the range is a recipe for a 47.90 short sale.

2.   The second bar of the day gaps lower, approximately to the planned entry.

3.   The stock moves smoothly lower over the course of more than an hour. The reversal bar triggers an exit and retraces almost 50% of the Baltimore Chop move. The stock proceeds to trade up, closing near the high of the day. RA demonstrates clearly that profits in hand need to be protected and taken at the first sign of trouble with this strategy.

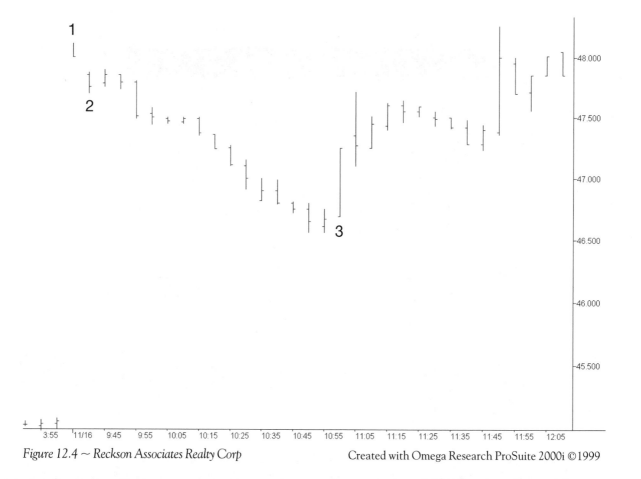

Figure 12.4 ~ Reckson Associates Realty Corp   Created with Omega Research ProSuite 2000i ©1999

Reckson Associates Realty Corp NYSE : RA	
11/02/2006	0.49
11/03/2006	0.39
11/06/2006	0.32
11/07/2006	0.27
11/08/2006	0.21
11/09/2006	0.50
11/10/2006	0.33
11/13/2006	0.60
11/14/2006	0.40
11/15/2006	0.50

Table 12.4.1 ~ 10 Day RA TR Values

Descriptive Statistics	
Mean	0.40
Standard Error	0.04
Median	0.40
Mode	0.50
Standard Deviation	0.12
Sample Variance	0.01
Kurtosis	-0.80
Skewness	0.03
Range	0.39
Minimum	0.21
Maximum	0.60
Sum	4.01
Count	10.00
Confidence Level (95%)	0.09

Table 12.4.2 ~ RA Summary Statistics

SUMMARY

The Baltimore Chop is a common pattern that occurs repeatedly on an almost daily basis. Once a trader is used to seeing the simple variations of the move, it becomes progressively easier to separate the good ones from the bad. Since most direct access trading software has provisions for finding gaps, it is just a matter of flipping charts to find the ones that are running into resistance and have the potential to make for a good fade.

CHAPTER 13

Breaking Ball

∙∙

… An off-speed pitch that curves.

The Breaking Ball pattern solves a problem that plagued me early in my trading career. The issue had to do with spotting intraday setups and getting into positions when a stock seemed to be running away from me. Too often, my entry would be the extreme tick of the day, and I would watch in disgust as everything turned around and moved against me. The dilemma with a quick intraday move is always whether to try boarding a moving train, or to wait and see if it is going to stop at the station. Too often, the outcome of jumping in the middle of a trend is whiplash as price reverses and sends the stock immediately toward the stop loss. The solution for me was to wait for the move to consolidate at the extreme of the initial range, and then take an entry in the direction of the move only if a break from the consolidation reasserted the initial trend.

The Breaking Ball pattern is very simple to spot. I use a 5-minute chart and start flipping a symbol list comprised of stocks trading above (longs) or below (shorts) their 20, 50, and 200 SMA's, with good ADX and DMI. I begin this process as soon as the market opens, and keep a scribbled list of everything that is moving in concert with my primary criteria.

The pattern can actually occur at any time during the day, but I like it best right off the open. The rules for longs and shorts are as follows:

1. The stock must make a large-range 5-minute move higher or lower.

2. Price consolidates in a narrow range with clearly identifiable highs and lows for at least three bars.

3. Entry is on a .10 - .15 break that clearly violates the consolidation. The stop is the opposite extreme of the consolidation range.

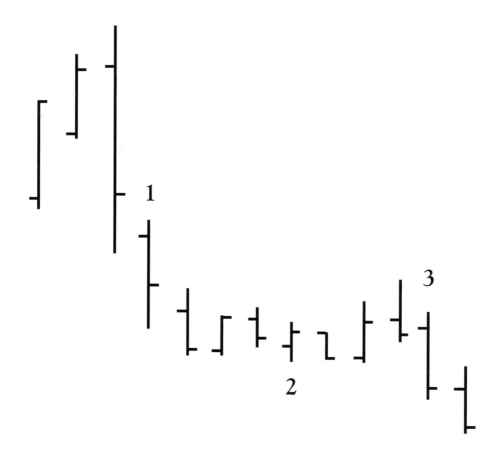

The focus of the Breaking Ball pattern is to scalp small profits, but it can sometimes yield impressive gains. Agilent Technologies Inc. (A) is a frequent mover. Here, the stock provides a good example of the Breaking Ball pattern in action.

1. A congestion zone is followed by a wide range move lower.

2. A three-bar consolidation range forms and triggers a short entry on the violation of the bottom of the channel.

3. The stock moves $0.13 lower and consolidates again.

4. By the end of trading, Agilent has generated $0.50 per share in intraday profits. Although each consolidation range breakout was only minimally profitable, the sum attained by staying with the move over the trading day added a nice gain on the session.

Figure 13.1 ~ Agilent Technologies, Inc.   Created with Omega Research ProSuite 2000i ©1999

Energizer Holdings, Inc. (ENR) was mentioned in my *Stocks to Watch* column frequently during 2006 and early 2007. When a stock is regularly on the watch list, it also pays to look at it intraday even if it did not present a pattern setup. Those days, which sometimes seem to offer no potential, can be full of good moves.

1. A sharp move off the open leads to a Breaking Ball consolidation range.

2. Price moves out of the pattern and begins to push higher.

3. After moving higher through several brief consolidations, ENR breaks the bottom of the final range triggering a trailing profit stop at $0.46 per share.

Figure 13.2 ~ Energizer Holdings, Inc.,   Created with Omega Research ProSuite 2000i ©1999

When a Breaking Ball position triggers, I will keep it open as long as it does not violate the parallel channel bar to the one that triggered the entry. In other words, if the entry is on the short side of the market, I will stop out on a violation of the upper bar of the consolidation range.

1. Millipore Corporation (MIL) forms a long Breaking Ball consolidation after an opening pop and reversal.

2. The stock triggers an entry and then reverses back into the channel. The top of the tighter secondary consolidation serves as the new stop.

3. The stock forms another consolidation range and tests a breech lower several times before breaking down in a waterfall move.

4. A reversal stop triggers an exit when two closing prices are taken out to the upside. MIL yields $0.90 per share in Breaking Ball profits.

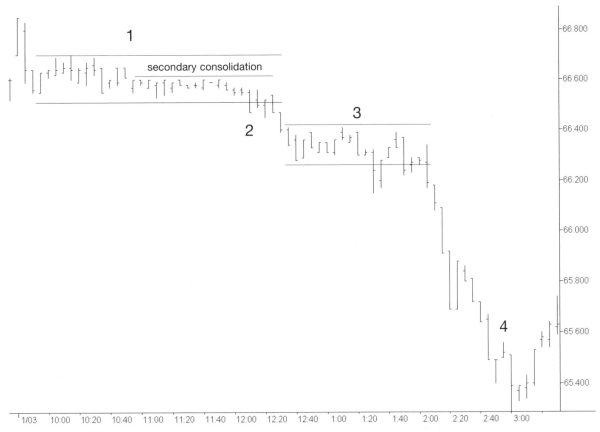

Figure 13.3 ~ Millipore Corporation   Created with Omega Research ProSuite 2000i ©1999

Airline stocks are very sensitive to fluctuations in oil prices. Couple wildly fluctuating fuel prices with earnings reports, contract negotiations or fare wars and the industry bellwethers can provide some interesting trading. AMR Corporation made many good moves intraday in late 2006 and early 2007. This is an example of the American Airlines parent reacting to fuel oil fluctuations.

1.   The stock gaps slightly lower and forms a Breaking Ball consolidation.

2.   An entry triggers as AMR breaks lower. The stock tacks on a $0.50 gain.

3.   AMR consolidates again, forming another Breaking Ball setup that also breaks to the downside.

4.   Another $0.60 in short side gains lead to an AMR reversal and Breaking Ball trailing stop at 32.77, $0.90 from the initial entry. The stock makes additional, tradeable pattern moves lower into the close.

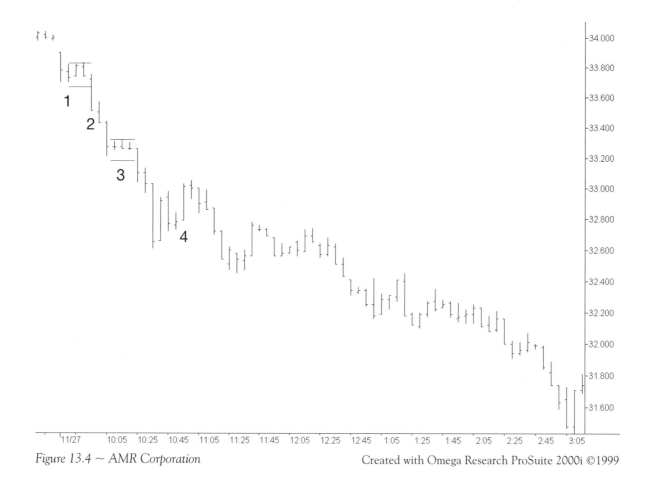

Figure 13.4 ~ AMR Corporation   Created with Omega Research ProSuite 2000i ©1999

Many of the traders in our TraderInsight.com War Room enjoy trading the sector holders due to their intraday range and volatility. The Semiconductor HOLDRs (SMH) is an exchange traded fund that is a favorite for many of the most active intraday market participants.

1. SMH gaps lower and makes a quick fade move higher. The HOLDR then reverses and starts moving lower.

2. After a 30-minute consolidation, SMH breaks the channel low and triggers a short sale. The stop-loss on the trade is at the violation of the top of the range. The HOLDR pulls back in and retests the Breaking Ball extremes.

3. Another Breaking Ball move violates the lower support of the channel. SMH begins trending lower.

4. Over the next few hours, SMH trends lower by as much as $0.50 per share.

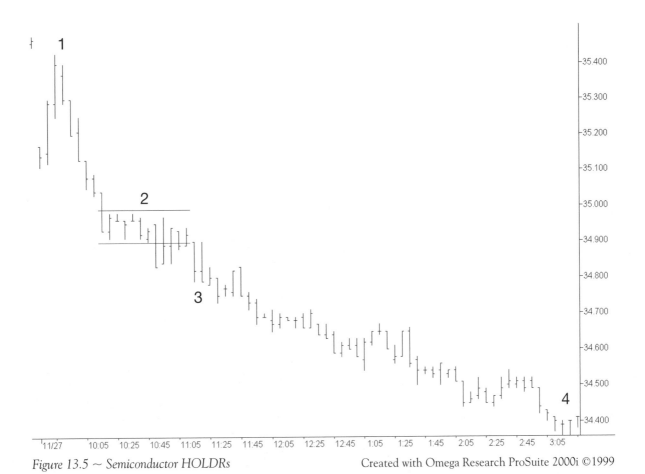

Figure 13.5 ~ Semiconductor HOLDRs   Created with Omega Research ProSuite 2000i ©1999

SUMMARY

When it comes to trading, simple is usually better. The Breaking Ball is about as simple as things get. What it lacks in sophistication, this pattern makes up for in reliability, and I will take the latter over the former any day. The key here is spotting the opportunities when they exist. The best means of accomplishing this is to develop a discipline of flipping through a list of stocks matching narrowly defined criteria and pulling only those setups that are perfect. Much like any entry, if you try to force something that is not there, the result will more likely be burned fingers than profitability.

CHAPTER 14

Checked Swing

....

… A split second decision by a batter not to follow through with a swing. If the swing has gone more than halfway around, the umpire can rule it a full swing, or strike.

The best intention of knocking the ball out of the park can be eliminated in the blink of an eye by a pitch that causes a batter to rethink his swing. A similar phenomenon occurs when a Fast Ball setup is thrown to the market and the broad response is to pass on the previous day's momentum and let the stock retrace a portion of the expansion move. The Checked Swing gives us an intraday entry opportunity just when we would have otherwise thought that a pattern was going to fail to hand us profits.

Pattern failures are a dissappointing fact of a trader's life. In the case of a failed Fast Ball setup, however, they can be the seeds of opportunity. The Checked Swing relies on the propensity of wide range days to be followed by additional volatility, even if the result is not follow-through. Basically, the trade is a means of anticipating the fear of traders who caught the tail end of the prior day's move and now feel that it is time to quickly head for the exit.

The criteria for longs and shorts are as follows:

1. The stock opens and trades in the direction of the previous day's range expansion high or low.

2. The Fast Ball pattern fails to break out, or breaks out and reverses. The stock then trades in a short consolidation shy of the previous day's range extreme.

3. Entry is a few ticks outside the consolidation range.

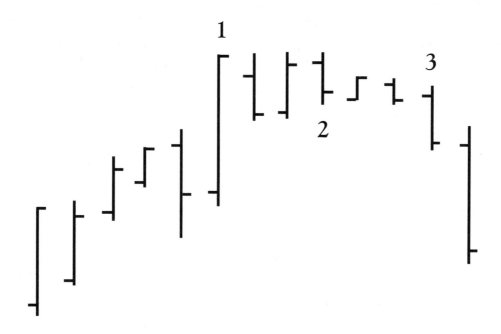

Thermo Electron Corp. (TMO) tends to trade in daily consolidation ranges and then push higher or lower on wide range. The stock provides Checked Swing reaction moves to these thrusts on a pretty regular basis.

1. TMO moves higher in a Fast Ball breakout that pushes the stock just above the pattern trigger price. The stock consolidates in an upward triangle.

2. A Checked Swing breakdown signals a Fast Ball failure and potential reversal move. The entry trigger is below the ascending trend line.

3. TMO trades lower by $0.30 and forms a Breaking Ball consolidation.

4. By the end of the session, the stock has traded down by $.075, yielding a good profit in place of the Fast Ball stop-loss.

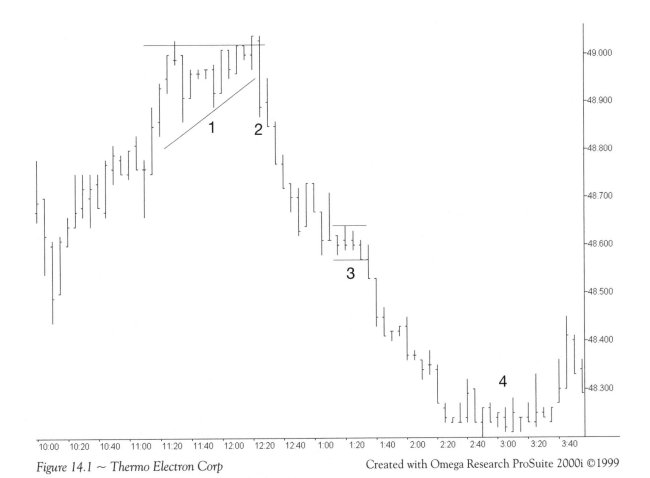

Figure 14.1 ~ Thermo Electron Corp   Created with Omega Research ProSuite 2000i ©1999

Bausch & Lomb Inc. (BOL) left a very wide range Fast Ball on expanded range and volume on December 13, 2006. I discussed the stock's inability to follow through on such large moves in my nightly *Stocks to Watch* column and was on the lookout for a reversal the following day. This trade demonstrates again the importance of becoming familiar with the personalities of a number of regularly traded stocks.

1.   A Checked Swing consolidation forms after BOL opens and triggers a Fast Ball entry.

2.   A move lower triggers a short sale reversal of the Fast Ball trade.

3.   BOL trades lower and reverses, yielding $0.50 on the move.

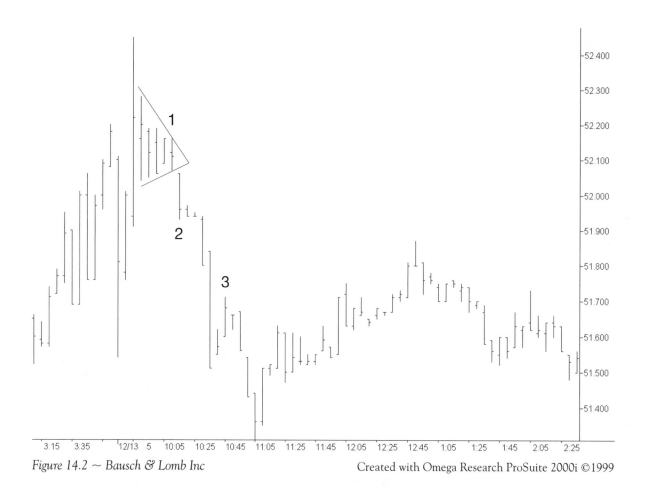

Figure 14.2 ~ Bausch & Lomb Inc   Created with Omega Research ProSuite 2000i ©1999

The Checked Swing pattern can generate waterfall moves. When these develop, the best trailing stop is usually a trendline. This allows a stock to make a normal series of pullbacks without generating early exits.

1. Exelon Corp. (EXC) gaps beyond its Fast Ball entry price and immediately forms a short Checked Swing consolidation.

2. A break through the bottom of the range triggers a short sale.

3. Waiting for a trend line violation has the trade open until a congestion range forms, yielding $0.60 per share.

Figure 14.3 ~ Exelon Corporation   Created with Omega Research ProSuite 2000i © 1999

Anglogold (AU) frequently participates in overreaction moves in the gold and mining markets. The stock is often gapped through pattern trigger prices, and has a tendency to reverse course as profit-takers or bottom-pickers rush in to capitalize on the extreme open. When these gap moves occur, we look for consolidations to form and break out early in the session.

1. AU is gapped up through the Fast Ball entry price and immediately starts a Checked Swing consolidation.

2. Thirty minutes pass and the stock breaks lower.

3. As the session progresses, AU follows its trend line lower into the close.

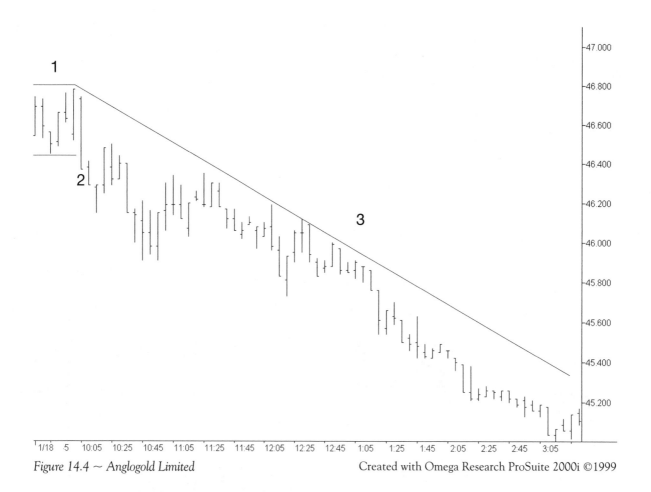

Figure 14.4 ~ Anglogold Limited   Created with Omega Research ProSuite 2000i ©1999

Capital One Financial (COF) provides a final example of the Checked Swing pattern as a means of handling contratrend moves after a Fast Ball gap open.

1. A booming open has COF well above the Fast Ball trigger price. The stock immediately starts selling off.

2. A consolidation pattern forms $0.20 above the previous session high.

3. A break through the bottom of the Checked Swing consolidation, and the bar closes into the Fast Ball range.

4. A trend stop closes the trade with $1 in profits.

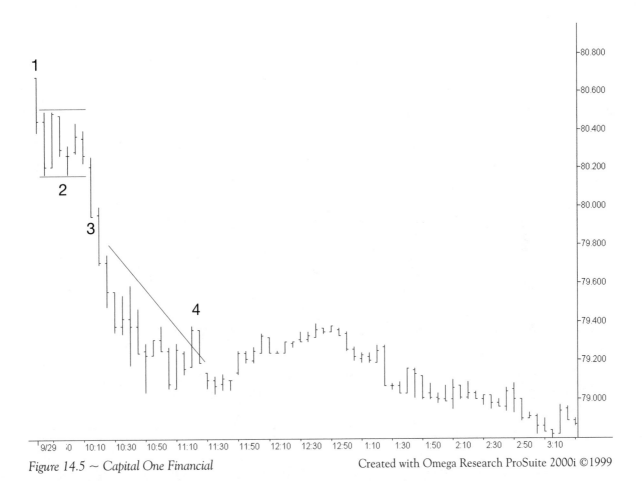

Figure 14.5 ~ Capital One Financial   Created with Omega Research ProSuite 2000i ©1999

SUMMARY

The Checked Swing gets us in scoring position when other market factors seem to be working against our plan. Although I always advocate sticking to the pre-planned trades, this one can be anticipated the night before and kept aside as a contingency. In those instances that play out, the pattern can provide quick profits with very limited risk.

SECTION IV
CLOSING THOUGHTS

CHAPTER 15

Keeping Score

··

…Procrastination is the art of keeping up with yesterday.
---Don [ald Robert Perry] Marquis

Every trader, no matter what his/her level of experience, will benefit by knowing what happened, when it happened and why. The problem for most of us is that we focus on the results and not the chain of events that led to them. By the time we realize that there is a problem, the only way we can figure out the cause is to go back and attempt to reconstruct history. Revisionist history is based on guessing about the cause of decisions and outcomes. Armed with these speculative hunches we go back to work and attempt to right the listing ship on the basis of our guess work. Contrast this with the practices of successful traders who have closets full of their log files for each and every trade. When something goes wrong, these people have an objective means of addressing the problem before it gets out of hand. When things go well, they can review their notes and create their daily plan with an emphasis on what works for them. In this chapter, I will show you an effective means of logging every planned and executed trade.

Keeping an accurate record of every trade that is planned and every trade that triggers is a prerequisite for success. You can try to survive in this business without going through the hassle of logging everything, but if that's your intention, then you may as well just burn your money one dollar at a time. I assure you, it will last longer, and at least you will be entertained and warm instead of frustrated and sick to your stomach.

The temptation for most traders is to log the big winners, log the trades that blow out, and forget about everything else. This practice results in 90% of activity being lost forever. To say that something in this business is unimportant because it is mundane borders on the ridiculous. Trading is not the thrill of victory and the agony of defeat. It is about going to work and making money. It often revolves around doing nothing. During much of the trading day, our hands serve us best as seat cushions. This is a profession that requires accute attention and focus on the details. A highly descriptive trade log is part of success.

I run a nightly trading service for a small list of subscribers. I started this as much to keep focus and discipline as I did in response to requests from traders to share my stock selections. Every night, I plan everything for the next trading session down to the last detail. I record entry triggers, logical profit targets, logical stop losses and all the anticipated areas of support and resistance that will be encountered during the day. I identify the sector with which each stock is most highly correlated and note the relative strength value associated with it in *Investors Business Daily*. I keep my plans in three ring binders and review them religiously to make sure that there is continuity in my approach to the work that I do.

I also keep a log file of every trade. I take a snapshot of the intraday chart and post it in a log file template. I mark the entry, support and resistance encountered, and the exit. I then write a brief commentary of what happened once the trade triggered. I do this for every trade, and often this means chronicling events that are as mundane as "we entered at 50.20, and the trade drifted slowly to our stop loss." For me, this is not tedium, it is necessity.

On the following pages, you will find some actual examples from my service and log files.

The following examples contain excerpts from

Tricks of the Trade
Peterson/Manz Trading
Trade Log February 2007

Trade Date
Tuesday, January 30, 2007

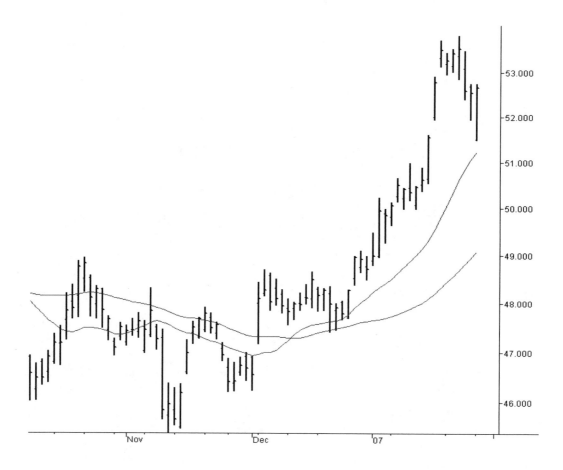

Symbol	ABT		Relative Strength	76
Description	Abbott Laboratories			
Pattern	Switch Hitter		Sector	Drugs
Position	Long		Support 2	51.07
Entry	52.85		Support 1	51.86
Stop	52.49		Pivot	52.31
Initial Target	53.38		Resistance 1	53.10
Ratio	1.47		Resistance 2	53.55

ABT

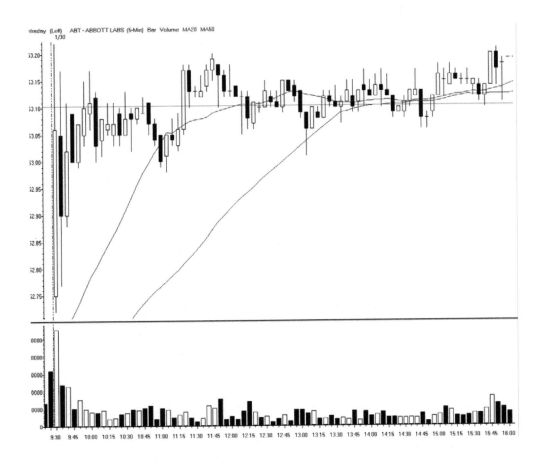

Abbott Laboratories triggered our long entry right off the open and traded within $0.20 of the initial profit target immediately. Julie ratcheted the trailing stop to just below breakeven, and we watched the stock consolidate right at R1 for a good part of the session. The stock made several wide oscillating moves over the course of the session and came close to stopping out a couple times. By the close, the stock was once again trading $0.20 under our target, which is exactly where an exit was triggered just prior to the bell.

Trade Date
Tuesday, January 30, 2007

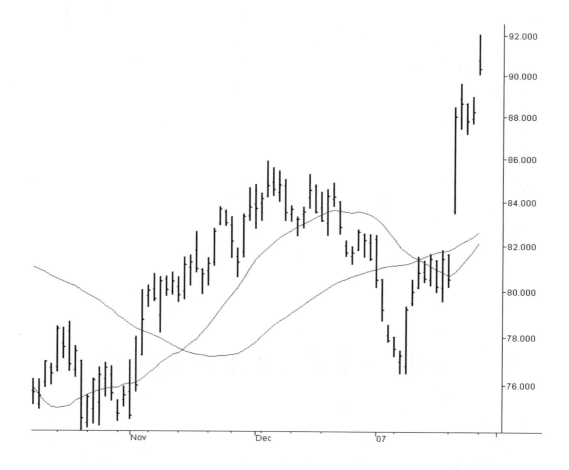

Symbol	JEC		Relative Strength	71
Description	Jacobs Engineering Group Inc			
Pattern	Infield Fly		Sector	Construction
Position	Short		Support 2	88.87
Entry	89.95		Support 1	89.60
Stop	90.52		Pivot	90.83
Initial Target	89.10		Resistance 1	91.56
Ratio	1.49		Resistance 2	92.79

JEC

Intraday (Left) JEC - JACOBS ENGR GROUP INC DEL (5-Min) Bar Volume MA20 MA50

Jacobs Engineering Group proved to be one of those very frustrating trades to-day. I was looking for a move down to multiday support at 89.10, but the stock stopped dead in its tacks at the S1 level and reversed. This represented a move of 50% to the target, and we trailed at $0.20 above the entry price for a scratch. We were trailed out for a small loss, and no re-entry opportunity presented itself.

Trade Date
Tuesday, January 30, 2007

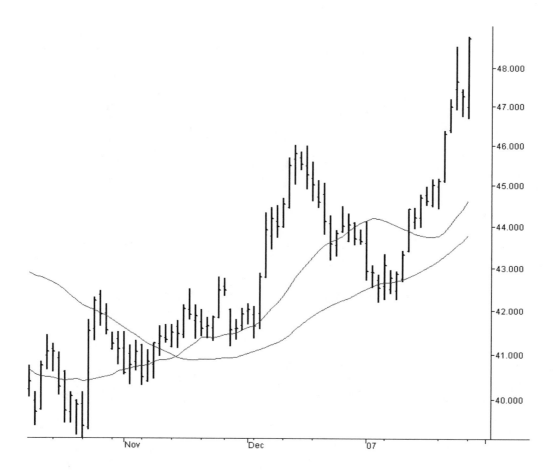

Symbol	TK	Relative Strength	81	
Description	Teekay Shipping Corp			
Pattern	Fast Ball	Sector	Shipping	
Position	Long	Support 2	45.97	
Entry	48.93	Support 1	47.37	
Stop	48.46	Pivot	48.10	
Initial Target	49.50	Resistance 1	49.50	
Ratio	1.21	Resistance 2	50.23	

TK

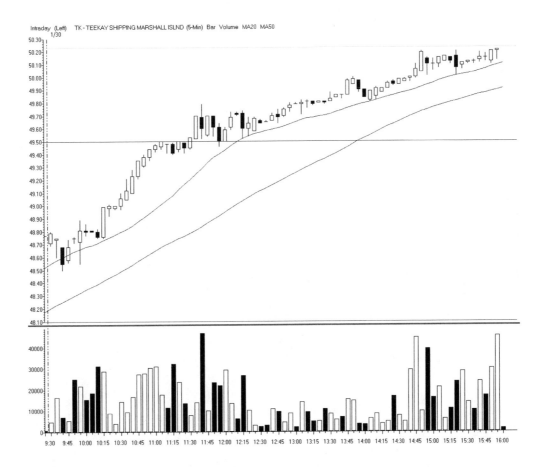

Intraday (Left)   TK - TEEKAY SHIPPING MARSHALL ISLND (5-Min) Bar Volume MA20 MA50

Teekay Shipping was the trade du jour. The stock opened and cleanly triggered our stated entry. A clean move to R1 (right around the initial target) was followed by a tight 30-minute consolidation that broke in our favor. The stock moved higher and reversed briefly to the initial target level, stopping out 50% of the position. Over the remainder of the day, TK moved higher closing at the extreme of the bar and putting in a nice extension to Monday's Fast Ball move. The extension put the move right at the R2 resistance level.

Trade Date
Tuesday, January 30, 2007

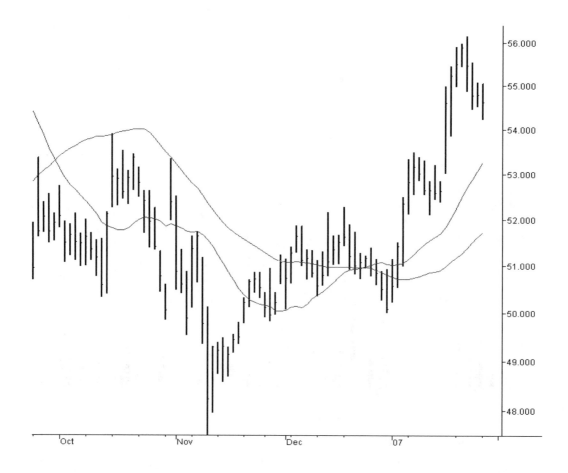

Symbol	BRL		Relative Strength	34
Description	Barr Pharmaceuticals Inc			
Pattern	Backdoor Slider / Extra Inning		Sector	Medical
Position	Short		Support 2	53.81
Entry	54.15		Support 1	54.18
Stop	54.45		Pivot	54.61
Initial Target	53.67		Resistance 1	54.98
Ratio	1.60		Resistance 2	55.41

BRL

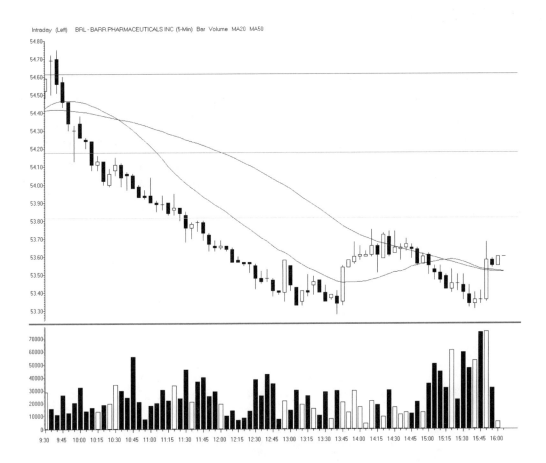

We used the low of the initial Backdoor Slider setup as an entry price on this one, as yesterday's close kept the spirit of the setup alive. Barr Pharmaceuticals opened and made a smooth trending move through the trigger price and to the initial target. The extension on the trade was a logical move to the daily 20-period simple moving average. The stock reversed course there for the first time in the session, and trailed out for a solid gain.

SUMMARY

I provided the examples in this section for the purpose of clarifying how I keep records. I suggest that you keep at least as much historical information of your trading activity as I do. The preference would be that you keep even more. There is no such thing as too much information when it comes to evaluating our own decisions and emotions. I hope that this section will give the reader a good place from which to start.

CHAPTER 16

Bottom of the 9th

... The end of the game.

Well, there you have it. You now possess some of the insight that a decade of trading professionally has brought me. The strategies I use are predominantly straight forward. Most trace their origins back to the earlier part of the last century when people like Gann were "writing the book" on technical analysis. Since that time, these setups have worked for traders through bull and bear markets, just as I am certain they will continue to generate profits in the future.

I rely on money management to keep my business profitable. I only plan to take a trade if it has at least a 1:1 profit/loss ratio. Before I accept even these odds of success, I make sure that the stock I am dealing with is heading in a direction supported by its fundamentals, and is unencumbered by intraday support and resistance.

I believe that consistency is the key to success as an equities trader, so I don't do a lot of flip-flopping when it comes to strategies. I trade the patterns in this book every day. If you find that they fit your personal psychology, then I would suggest that you add them to your repertoire slowly. Get to know each strategy and make sure it makes sense to you prior to adding additional ones. For additional examples of the setups, check our website

TraderInsight.com regularly and focus on the *Stocks to Watch* column and the *Nightly Wrap*. There you will find daily examples of the *Around The Horn* patterns my wife Julie and I are currently trading. You can also look over our shoulder in the *War Room*, an interactive community full of educational opportunities and live commentary from a variety of well-known professional traders.

If you are new to this business, I suggest that you read everything you can. Attend seminars, watch educational programs about trading, and scour the internet until you find a methodology that you think suits you. Every one of us can find a method that will help us become a successful trader. Not one of us can do so by blindly following the first methodology that comes along. Make sure that the fit between your belief structure and that of the system you are adopting is tight. Only then will you be able to trade confidently and in a manner that increases your probabilities for success.

I know from personal experience what you are up against in the profession you have chosen. If you find your own way to rise above it all, I am confident that you will see this as the best decision you ever made. I wish you good luck on your journey.

Good Trading,

Adrian Manz

Appendix

Tools of the Trade

The reliability of the equipment and software a trader uses are paramount in achieving success. I have found that of all the problems we face in trying to deal with the markets, technology ranks number 1 on the list of frustrations. Over the years, I have managed to put together a stable platform that includes software and hardware from vendors I consider to be the best in the business.

Our war room is pictured below. As you can see, we use eleven screens to monitor the markets over the course of the day. This gives us plenty of room to watch what each of the stocks in the nightly service is doing.

We use two Dell workstations running twin, dual core, XEON processors at the highest clock speed available today. Each of the Dell machines is loaded with two gigabytes of RAM, and more hard disk space than I will likely use in a lifetime. I am a firm believer in headroom, and the machine you make your living with should be a best- in-class, highly reliable product.

I use Omega Research ProSuite 2000i for analytical work. The data is fed in real time via satellite by DTN. DTN provides reasonably priced real-time data and is without question one of the best data feeds in the industry.

My brokerage software is the industry standard product RealTick. We clear through a variety of firms, but my favorite is TerraNova Trading. I have been so satisfied with their customer service and product offerings over the years, that they are now the primary firm through which I clear transactions.

Our backup feed and brokerage is TradeStation Technologies. They have done a very good job of porting the capabilities of the 2000i product into an intraday execution platform. The new product, while no replacement for the 2000i line, in terms of nightly chart scanning capabilities, has proven itself reliable and consistent, and is capable of fully automating a trading strategy.

Finally, I use a product called the *SortWizard* to monitor the market and search for new setups during the trading session. The *SortWizard* is a stock screening tool designed to be used in conjunction with the RealTick datafeed. In seconds, and without symbol list size limitations, I can scan the entire market in real-time to generate stock trading lists that meet specific criteria. There are many speed, efficiency, and convenience features built in to make analysis and use seamless with RealTick. I use the Plus Version which allows me to write my own customized formulas, selecting reference information from a comprehensive list of data fields and a custom database. This product reduces scanning the market for setups to a single step during the trading day. Once the trigger events have been set, the software displays the results real-time. In addition, *SortWizard* allows for the creation of baskets of stocks to scan rather than forcing you to scan the entire market. This limits the output to equities that I actually have an interest in trading rather than every stock that meets a pattern criteria. The company has released a custom module that finds the patterns in *Around The Horn*. The software and the module are available at *TraderInsight.com*.

Peterson/Manz Trading, Inc
Around The Horn
Trading Service

Each night, I select what I consider to be the best *Around The Horn* setups for the next trading session. My subscribers receive the exact same list of entries and exits that I trade from each day. If you would like a free two week trial to the service, please copy and fax the form below to (310) 230-7657. You may also send an email requesting a trial to trials@traderinsight.com. The number of subscriptions available is very limited to prevent liquidity problems in the equities we trade. If we receive more requests for trials or subscriptions than can be reasonably accomodated, you may be placed on a waiting list.

If you elect to keep the service after the trial period ends, the cost is $195.00 per month or $1,950.00 annually. We accept MasterCard, Visa and American Express.

Full Name _____

Email Address _____

Street Address 1 _____

Street Address 2 _____

City _____ State _____ Zip _____

Telephone _____

Facsimile _____

Please send my subscription to my (check one):

Online Retrieval (standard) ☐   Fax ☐

Email ☐

About The Author

Dr. Adrian Manz earns his living as a professional analyst and stock trader. A successful professional equities trader for nearly a decade, he is the author of two books on the subject and the publisher of the Intraday Trading Plan, a nightly blueprint for the actions he plans to take in the markets on the following day. Dr. Manz is president of Peterson/Manz Trading Inc., and the co-founder of TraderInsight.com and is dedicated to providing trader education to anyone who is looking to add a new view of the markets to their repertoire. He is a regular public speaker at trading events and is frequently interviewed about his trading style on radio and the Web. Dr. Manz is a graduate of the prestigious Peter F. Drucker Graduate School of Management and the School of Behavioral and Organizational Sciences at Claremont Graduate School. He and his wife Dr. Julie Peterson-Manz live and work in Pacific Palisades, California.

Find Great Around The Horn Trading Setups Every Day at TraderInsight.com

Want my daily watch list of stocks? Join me at TraderInsight.com.

Every evening, I post *Around the Horn* stock trading setups at TraderInsight.com. At TraderInsight.com, you can listen to my nightly audio commentary and read my daily watch list to help you with the next day's trading. These stocks are the very same ones that I'll be looking to trade. Go to TraderInsight.com today, and be sure to sign up for my free newsletter. I'll email you new trading ideas, setups and actionable market information.

Adrian Manz
TraderInsight.com

TraderInsight.com
Strategy, Discipline, Results